Cricket Down The Lane
A History of Morecambe Cricket Club

By John Butler

2010

Published by Rel8 Media
PO Box 29145, Dunfermline, Fife, KY12 7WJ

© Rel8 Media and John Butler, 2010

British Library in Publication Data.
A catalogue record for this volume is available from the British Library.

ISBN 978-0-9555307-3-9

Contents

About The Author

John Butler is a life member of Morecambe Cricket Club having been associated with the club from the inaugurral formation of the clubs junior section.

A 'Sand Grown Un' he was brought up within a 'six hit' of the ground on Woodhill Lane in his early years.

Educated at Balmoral Secondary School in its transition to Heysham High School, he has witnessed the clubs turbulent past from the mid seventies to the present day and is well qualified to chronicle the clubs rise to the forefront of the local community.

He has played with the clubs senior teams since 1973 with the exception of the 1990 season in which he played for Settle CC in the Ribblesdale League. The Northern League website records him having taken over 650 league wickets . Having retired from playing in 2000 he has played an active part in the recruitment of the clubs professional and cricket administration, over the last decade and is currently a Northern League Umpire.

Acknowledgements

I am indebted to the following people for the loan of photographs and reference material for inclusion in this publication.

Mr. Brian Paton
Mr. Jeff Forrest
Mr. Ken & Mr. Doug Youren
Millom Folk Museum
Barnsley Chronicle
Roger Sandham
Ian Hanson
Frank Henry
Peter Kyles
Ashwell Prince
Surrey CCC
Phil McCormack, Whitehaven CC
Brooksbank Family,
Whitehaven Record Office,
Keighley Record Office,

A special thanks to Mike Latham for his guidance, advice, and encouragement in making everything come together and lastly to my wife Pam for her support during the long process of researching the book together with putting up with the 'white box' I promise it will now be removed from the front room !

Bibliography

The History of the North Lancashire and District Cricket League, Bryn Trescatheric.
The History of the Lancaster Cricket Club, J.J. Gilchrist.
Cricket by the Lune, Tom Alderson.
'See The Conquering Hero' Story of the Lancashire League 1892-1992 by Dave Edmundson
History of Darfield CC by I.M.Randerson
History of Kendal CC 1836-1935, James Clarke.
One Hundred Years of The Ribblesdale Cricket League 1892-1992, Alan West.
Of Smittle Pots and Sticky Buns, John Glaister.

Together with the numerous newspaper publications on microfilm at The Harris Museum, Preston, plus the local libraries at Morecambe, Lancaster, Kendal, and Barrow.

Preface

The idea of a history of the club developed from the Centenary brochure produced in 1989 together with the other numerous books published to mark the history of many other clubs. As a contributor to the Centenary Brochure I realized there must be more stories to be told about the history and development of the club together with its many personalities that have graced both the playing and administrative roles

Although it is now over 20 years since that publication information has been collated in spells over the years as it was clearly evident from the start that the clubs own records were extremely limited. The local newspapers carried fairly extensive reports of matches going back a long way although certain years were missing. Details of Annual Meetings and other events of significance were generally well reported.

In general terms I have tried to explain the development of the club. World events sometimes dictate the course of certain actions but it is the parts played by individuals which have been of paramount importance in shaping the club's direction.

I hope some of the names of past players and officials will generate interest with some of the present inhabitants of the town to speculate if some of these past members are relatives of the current generation.

Nevertheless the main purpose was to provide a historical record of Morecambe Cricket Club and for that reason it is written mainly for the members past, present, and future. I hope other cricket followers will find the book of some interest.

Message from the President

I deem it to be a great privilege and honour to be writing a few words as President of Morecambe Cricket Club in this publication chronicling the history of the club.

A great amount of change has happened since the inaugural meeting to set up a cricket club in Morecambe well over a hundred years ago. Many players have graced the Morecambe teams since those early years and all would be suitably impressed with the improvements that have taken place over the recent years.

The clubhouse has been made into one of the best in the league and the playing surface is well received by visiting players and officials as an excellent venue.

This has not always been the case however and the efforts to build a club that is respected not only within the circle of North West England but in further outposts of the cricketing world has taken many years. As the book details the efforts to secure the ground, the clubs nearly ever present financial problems in its early years, and a resilience to overturn a proposal for the club to be wound up all have been overcome and we are now able to record our achievements for future generations.

I have had the privilege of having many friends within the cricketing circle of Morecambe Cricket Club and raise my glass to members past and present and the future of our club.

Yours

Charles E Clough

A Message from Ashwell Prince . . .

Arriving in Manchester in the early part of April 1999 to embark on a season of club cricket as the overseas professional of MCC, I really did not know what to expect. The only two things I had been assured of was that it would still be very cold and wet in the north west of England and that the pitches would be extremely slow compared to what I was used to back home.

I was greeted at the airport by one of the clubs committee members at the time, Mervyn Evans. Merv was instrumental and I must add persuasive in making the deal happen, as he was doing all the negotiations on behalf of the club. I say persuasive as I was on the verge of signing for another club in the Ribblesdale League, but he would not have any of that and started selling the club and town to me. Born and bred in the coastal city of Port Elizabeth and having moved to Cape Town in the summer of 1997 I had always lived on the coast. Merv was fully aware of all of this and by the time he was done trying to convince me to join Morecambe, the place sounded like a seaside resort in the Caribbean.

Anyone who has ever been to the little seaside town of Morecambe will know it is a resort of years gone by; none the less, I was a young ambitious cricket professional so the less distractions the better. During the drive from Manchester up to Morecambe, Merv gave me a brief history lesson about the club. Apart from all the big names who have previously represented the club as the overseas player, the only other thing that stood out very prominently was the rivalry between Morecambe and the neighbouring town of Lancaster. It became very clear from the outset how important this particular fixture was to both teams. It sounded as though nothing else mattered, even if we ended second bottom, as long as they were last and we beat them.

Over my two seasons spent at the club we certainly ended a few positions above them on both occasions but I think we probably ended up sharing the derby results with one or two rained out. Nights out after a derby would often depend on the result of the match, after a win it would definitely be Lancaster and needless to say after a loss it would be a quiet night in Morecambe.

On the subject of nights out, I actually preferred Morecambe rather than Lancaster, not because I am biased but simply because I don't drink and preferred going out and having a dance instead. Whilst most of our lads preferred a night pub hopping in Lancaster, you would probably find myself and a few others on the dance floor in 'The Kings Arms' a small hotel /pub/nightclub on the bay. We had some very good nights in there, and just before getting a cab home in what soon became a little tradition we always stopped off at 'Shaheeniho's' for a chicken kebab.

During my two years at the club we had quite good results on the field and whilst we lacked consistency in the league format we were quite the opposite in the cups. I suppose you could say we were the type of team who could beat anybody on the day but the reverse could also happen. Without a doubt the highlight of my two years at the club was in the season of 1999 when we won one of the cup competitions in a final at the club's Woodhill Lane ground against a much more experienced, consistent and probably most feared side in the league at the time, Chorley. The original match was rained out the week before after one innings with us bundled out for little over one hundred. The following week was a totally different story. The sun was out, the 'Lane' was packed and we were well 'UP FOR IT' as they say. We had had some fiery games against them in the league and we were not about to give an inch. We may have been a lot younger and less experienced than them, but we also had some big units in our team and were certainly not going to be intimidated by them.

If my memory serves me correctly they batted first and scored somewhere near 180. This kind of total would not be a problem under normal circumstances to knock off, but these were anything but normal circumstances. It was a cup final in front of a full house and they had arguably the best bowling pro in the league in Josh Marquet. He was a big strapping Aussie who loved bowling a bumper and intimidating the opposition with his big frame. Having played first team league cricket since the age of 14 back home, coming up against the likes of Brett Shultz, Rod McCurdy (another Aussie) and a few others at that age, I certainly wasn't taking a backward step against Josh Marquet. I played one of my best innings for the club that day, something in the 70's if I remember correctly, coming in at no 3 but when I got out, there was still a bit to be done. Needless to say, the boys put on the finishing touches and we had a great night celebrating at the club.

The two years spent at the club has most certainly stood me in good stead for what was to follow. As a young professional you very soon become aware of the pressure on you as you are the only paid player in the team and people obviously expect more. This teaches one responsibility as you soon learn that you have to find a way to deal with these pressures. When things are not going that well on the field, it can be very lonely when you are a long way away from home in a foreign country, far away from friends and family and support structures that you would normally have at home.

It was during these kinds of moments where a special friendship was struck. During my two years at the club I lived with one of the players, Graham (Chubby G) Lee. Whilst I regard all at the club to be my friends I obviously formed stronger relationships with some. Living with Graham meant we obviously spent a lot more time together and formed a stronger bond. We became very good friends and still are to this day and in fact our friendship is so great that Graham flew all the way to Cape Town to be the best man at my wedding. "Thank you very much for your support over the years buddy, I really hold our friendship dear to my heart".

At this stage I would like to thank all the people who have helped me have a wonderful and unforgettable two years at the club. In no particular order, Mr & Mrs Ian Hanson (chairman at the time), Tommy Clough (current club captain and close friend), Bob, Trish, Andrew and Laura Mashiter (close friends), Graham's parents (Geoff and Mary-Rose), Phil Thornton (club captain at the time), Merv Evans, Mark Woodhead, the Pedder family, Karl Hanson and family, Peter (Curts) Stephens and all the players with whom who I had the pleasure of sharing a dressing room.

I wish you all the very best for future) seasons, hope to see you all soon.

God bless

Ash.

Chapter One—What The Victorians Did For Us . . .

Records chronicling the history of Morecambe Cricket Club are few as many of the club's records were destroyed when the old pavilion was vandalised and its roof was in such poor repair the rain cascaded through to destroy the documents.

Through a mixture of sources I have been able to put together a fragmented history of the club's early years gathering more recent information on the latter years as new technology preserved these records.

The *Lancaster Gazette* records the first match with Morecambe players on Wednesday 31st May 1854. This was a two innings game at a Morecambe venue near to the railway station with ten players on each side. For the record the scores reported were Morecambe 50 and 84 and Lancaster 44 and 7. A shortage of Morecambe players meant that Lancaster loaned players to equal the sides.

A return game was played on the 15th August 1855 at Lancaster when the Morecambe novices proved something of a surprise in beating the Lancastrians by 123 runs to 51. A record of the game details the Morecambe men in the team. Lancaster, an established club, regarded themselves as one of the county's top club sides. In 1859 a victory was achieved again by the Morecambe team, winning by seven wickets in a two innings game. From Mr. JJ Gilchrist's book 'The History of The Lancaster Cricket Club' published in 1910 the result was reported as follows: *'The antagonists of the Lancaster club were the ever famous Morecambe XI who through having experienced many vicissitudes of fortune, have at length established an unrivalled notoriety, having on every match which they have played during the last and present seasons'.* It is hoped the Morecambe team celebrated their victory in style as the club would have to wait until 1911 before defeating Lancaster again, this time in a North Lancashire League match won by 165 runs to 100.

In those early days cricket was more of social event with no rigid restrictions over playing time. Bands, bunting and underhand bowling, with suppers or dinners to follow the matches were its accompaniments.

A *Lancaster Guardian* report dated June 1874 made the following historical pronouncement: *'A game of cricket was played on Wednesday in a field on the Heysham Road between eleven of Morecambe and the same number of Shap. The day was very unfavourable for cricket as showers fell at intervals during the whole of the day. Despite the weather, however one innings was played and the game resulted in a Morecambe victory by sixteen runs. Shap scoring 75 and Morecambe 91'*

Cricket was then played occasionally with no established club and only irregular friendly matches up to the late 'eighties.

During these years Morecambe became a flourishing watering place as the Railway brought in the workers from Lancashire and Yorkshire towns who for once a year broke away from the smog and industrial backdrop for a holiday at the seaside. In 1850 the completion of the line from West Riding to Morecambe was complete and with it the opportunity for men to obtain work in a developing town which had taken its name from the surrounding bay encompassing Poulton, Bare and Torrisholme.

In 1854 Morecambe had two railway stations, one at the pier head and another one at the present location of The Platform previously known as the Promenade Station. The railway was built not to bring tourists to the sea but to enable goods and trade to be transferred from the pier we now know as The Stone Jetty. This was because the Lune was beginning to silt-up and prevent large ships landing on St George's Quay. There is no doubt that Yorkshiremen, who had come to live and work in the prospering watering place, were mainly responsible for the club's inception.

On Friday 7th June 1889 a meeting was held at the King's Arms Hotel, Morecambe for the purpose of forming the 'Morecambe Cricket Club'. A further meeting resumed ten days later and officials elected were the following: President: Mr. E Gorrill, Hon/Sec Treasurer: Mr. T Kitching, Committee: The Rev W Disney, WJ Cross, RGW Howson, J Tilly, EW Pemberton, and T Birkett. The Reverend JFW Drury who was Curate at the St Barnabas Church was unanimously elected the first captain of the Morecambe Cricket Club.

Members numbered 52 and in the first year the club made a profit of £11 13s 6d. Mr. RGW Howson was a well respected figure within the expanding resort and one of the main movers in founding the club. Mr. Howson was born in Wray. He lived at 1 Craven Terrace, Morecambe working as a bank manager in the resort. His unfortunate death in 1905 was a huge blow to the club.

Details of the other founding officials in 1889 are limited but we do know Birkett was aged 30 at the time, born in Kendal, and living at 2 Highfield Terrace, working as a plasterer. Another plasterer was WJ Cross aged 33, born in Lancaster, and living at 15 Edward Street.

Secretary and Treasurer Mr. Thomas Kitching was to give invaluable service to the club up until his death in 1934. A life member, he played until he was well past the age of 60 and for many years he was in business on the Promenade near the Clock Tower as a jeweller and fancy goods dealer.

The club arranged to play at the Summer Gardens. This was an area that is currently occupied by Regent Park and The Gardens attracted huge crowds at its peak. A large Italian style pavilion in red brick and sandstone housed a large ballroom with refreshment facilities could hold a massive 10,000 people. On Easter Sunday in 1879 4,200 visitors went through the gates. The Gardens held athletic competitions such as wrestling with large prizes attracting competitors from the Lake District were the sport was prevalent. Lawn Tennis, Croquet, and Bowling Greens were freely available. Horse Racing was another crowd puller and it was indeed in the centre of the large racecourse that the club's first game was played at the ground at the end of June that year.

According to the club's centenary brochure this was against Halton. However, a report on the 'Ups and Downs of Local Cricket' from 'The Visitor ' in 1935 details the first game against the Lancaster Bank. The Summer Gardens covered thirty acres and pulled in a huge number of visitors. Advertising each week on the front page of the local press, the 'Gardens' weekend's attractions advert always included a reference to cricket being played on the site. The main reason for its decline was the opening of the 'Winter Gardens' and in 1890 an extraordinary general meeting was called by the directors of the company to consider voluntary liquidation. This was the club's first indication that finding a permanent home to play cricket in Morecambe was going to be an issue for club officials over the next 100 years.

After completing its first season in 1889 the club stated at the AGM it was to look for a professional. A number of applicants were considered and approached after which a professional by the name of Hoggard was recruited. Hoggard lasted just the first few weeks of the 1890 season which then saw Jack Weatherall as the club's professional. In his first match against the Lancaster Bank the side sustained a two run defeat but Weatherall had the excellent return of 9 overs, 3 maidens, 13 runs, 8 wickets. During that first season he took 99 wickets at 6.17 runs each. Little do we know of Weatherall except that he is recorded as playing some Minor Counties cricket for Durham in the early 1900's.

The club had a fixture list which through the advent of the railway resulted in games against Skipton, Bradford Wanderers, Silsden, Manchester Zingari, and Baildon Green. Against Galgate, the Morecambe side included three members of the clergy: Reverend JFW Drury, Rev W Robinson and the Rev TT Lancaster. In addition against Baildon Green the side included Rev J Burrows.

The Summer Gardens limped along with the club having to pay a rent on the site which was a huge burden on its finances. The local press reported prior to the 1891 season that the company was raising, leveling, and re-turfing a large tract of ground for cricket in the Summer Gardens and this was anticipated to be ready for the Whitsuntide weekend. The report went on to say the ground should prove to be one of the finest cricket grounds in the north. A compilation of fixtures had been secured and from the list was a large number of home games against Yorkshire teams while home and away fixtures against Caton, Settle, Bentham, Windermere, Lancaster, Carnforth and Kendal were arranged.

Following Weatherall's fine efforts in 1890 the club continued with a professional and it was reported that: '*A competent professional and groundsman has been secured in Mr. Ellis Town from the neighborhood of Bradford whose abilities as an all-round cricketer are attested by Mr. Tom Emmett of the Yorkshire County Eleven and other well known authorities.*' Town was in fact born in Halifax and professionals engaged in those days were expected to be to be an expert in groundsmanship as well as being an accomplished player. In the 1891 census Ellis Town was living in Keighley and registered as a labourer working in one of the town's mills. In 1895 he played one game for Cheshire in the Minor Counties Championship and in the next two years (1896 and 1897) became professional at Ramsbottom in the Lancashire League.

The first game of the season in 1891 was lost away to Caton although

Town was missing, as yet to take up his position. Very few details exist of the team's performances throughout that season although victory by 20 runs in one game against Bradford Wanderers was noted with Town returning an analysis of 8-12 with the ball. Limited records show Town played just the one season but in August the Lancaster Guardian reported a guest player for Morecambe in the victory against Carnforth. A Emmett of the Bradford club took six wickets for nine runs as Carnforth scored just 45 and were defeated by the home side's 49 for five wickets.

Considering the earlier press report referring to Tom Emmett this was probably his son Arthur who resided in Keighley with his family near to where Town lived. Tom Emmett had played for Yorkshire and England, finishing playing with the White Rose county in 1888. Arthur Emmett went on to play three first-class games for Leicestershire in 1902.

It appeared that the groundwork was not a success as the *Lancaster Guardian* reported in August: ' *The Lancaster First Eleven were disengaged on Saturday. The fixture down for decision on that day was the return match with Morecambe, but the Morecambe ground is – well, certainly not the best in the world, and especially when the wickets are hard, the ball gets up in a way most dangerous to batsmen, this being particularly the case when a fast bowler is operating. During the past fortnight or three weeks two men have I understand been hurt through the ball getting up in this way, one of them seriously. Under these circumstances it is not very astonishing that the Lancastrians declined to play on the Morecambe ground unless it was found to be in a better condition than usual. They offered however to play the match at Lancaster if a date convenient to both clubs could be agreed upon. The Morecambe Committee agreed that the action of the Lancaster Committee was reasonable and as there ground was not in any better condition on Saturday the match was not played. So far no other date has been fixed, but it is probable that the engagement will be carried out on the Lancaster ground some Wednesday afternoon.'*

In 1892 the club inevitably moved grounds to a field of which *The Visitor* reported *'a portion they were at once to re-lay; it being understood the club is to be re-organised'*. This ground location is difficult to visualise from limited map availability but given the old Morecambe Rugby League team played in a similar area and further newspaper reports about spectators not paying but sitting on a wall to watch the cricket it seems probable that the ground would be near the end of the current Northumberland Street.

That season the club entered the Lancaster & District League coming third in its first season. It is at this point in the club's history that one of its most successful players joined the club. Born at Ilkley in 1871 John Brooksbank was to become a leading player in the forthcoming years up to the outbreak of the First World War. In 1897 Brooksbank was reported as working at Williamson's in Lancaster and in his first match he took 7-13 against Caton. At the end of the season he won the club's bowling averages with 31 wickets at 3.06. He consistently continued to turn in performances making him the mainstay of the team.

The AGM of 1893 reported a deficit on the season of £60 mainly due to the purchase of a roller, bringing the club's debt to £148. The club continued to struggle on and somewhat against the financial reports we have read Jack Weatherall was to return as professional. Since his earlier appointment Weatherall had been with the Chadderton (Oldham) club and it was reported he was recruited as *'he was not only a sterling player but for his invariable good humour and courtesy.'*

The club continued its nomadic existence by leaving the Lancaster and District League after the 1893 season and reverted to playing fixtures on a casual basis against teams of variable strengths. The North Lancashire and District League had been formed in 1892 and the club was still playing these founder member clubs such as Kendal, Dalton and Lancaster, together with the County Asylum who had a short membership of the North Lancashire League.

In 1896 the club finished the season under the captaincy of F Tilly playing sixteen games, two of which were abandoned, winning five, losing six, and drawing three. The AGM reported a loss on the season of £14 3s 5d with Brooksbank winning the club's batting, bowling and fielding awards.

A remarkable game in 1897 against Carnforth resulted in a defeat for Morecambe by one run. When Carnforth were all out for 15 with Brooksbank taking five wickets including a hat-trick, a victory seemed a formality but Morecambe subsided to 14 all out losing their last seven wickets for one run.

Keeping cricket afloat in the town was epitomized by the report of the match against Carnforth in ' *The Visitor'* in May 1898. *'There was a capital attendance of spectators during the afternoon, probably 200 persons witnessing the match but unfortunately for the club only 23 of this number thought it worth their while to pay for the privilege of seeing the home team gain a pronounced victory over the visitors'.*

Morecambe Cricket Club, 1902

The report went on to explain how spectators could stand outside the perimeter of the ground and watch the game without paying. The report even tried to shame some of these people although drawing the line by naming them it detailed the following: *'On the wall contained about half a dozen well known land and property owners, two or three independent gentlemen, a member of the local district council and a would be member too, a builder or two and a host of other well known people whose names would form interesting reading matter'.*

To no avail, however, was the reporter's blacklist and the AGM of 1898 reported a deficit of £50.10s.6d. Jack Weatherall is recorded as playing in the 1898 and 1899 season but if this is in a capacity as the club professional is doubtful. In 1898 Weatherall took 54 wickets at 7.79, Brooksbank 40 at 9.27, but a young man by the name of Archie Sutcliffe took 13 wickets at 8.53 and scored 168 runs. Sutcliffe was a plasterer's labourer, born in Idle, Yorkshire and living at Alexandra Road in the town. In August 1905 he was awarded a benefit game. This appeared to be the tradition for local players who had not only given valuable service to a club but also performed admirably over the years.

The club had enough members to form a second team and this team entered the Lancaster and District League in 1898 and continued membership up to and including the 1903 season.

Major change was around the corner as the club moved to its present ground Woodhill Lane for the 1900 season. Despite never having a financially stable footing since its formation the club moved to its new ground and in early February the *Morecambe and Heysham Times* printed an illustration of the proposed new pavilion from a drawing by Mr. S Wright.

The article went on to describe the *'handsome and commodious pavilion'* in detail *'The Pavilion is to contain three rooms on the ground floor .The two side rooms are to be used as dressing rooms for the playing teams. The middle room will serve as a refreshment-room. Over one of these side rooms is a spacious sitting-room open at the front which will command an uninterrupted view of the field of play. The new premises are to contain seating accommodation for some 150 or 200 persons. The Pavilion will be raised from 6ft to 8ft from the ground on a rubble wall, and this rise of eight foot at the front will be broken by terraces on which seats will be placed.'*

Mr. John Edmondson was to be the contractor and the pavilion was to cost £500. On Saturday May 19th 1900 before the team were due to play Lancaster the pavilion was officially opened by Councillor John Gardner J.P. A total of £75 had already been subscribed to the building fund and with the advent of the new facilities it was hoped the club would grow in stature.

Captain for the 1900 season was Mr. Samuel Palmer M.A. Palmer was born in Cambridgeshire in 1854 and educated at Perse School and Corpus Christi College and gained an honours degree in classics. In 1878 he became classical master at St Bees School near Whitehaven. Leaving St Bees he came to Morecambe to work as The Headmaster of a private school at 'Olicana House'. This building is on the corner of St Margaret's Road and Marine Road. Palmer came to the club with a rich sporting pedigree as the local newspaper reported he was a triple blue in the hurdles race, long jump, and 100 yards. He had excelled as a footballer having played for Notts County, played rugby for the Cumberland team when he was with the Whitehaven club, and had played cricket for Cambridgeshire. For many years he had been interested in church work and in 1902 he became an ordained deacon and priest by the Bishop of Manchester. From 1902 to 1904 he was curate at the Parish Church, Poulton-le-Sands.

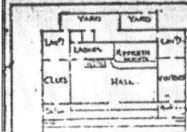

Morecambe Cricket Club: Pavilion. 1900.

The Morecambe Cricket Club's New Pavilion.

The Old Pavilion, Morecambe Cricket Club

In 1902 the town achieved borough status and chose as its motto *Beauty Surrounds: Health Abounds* and with those two undeniable claims the town went from strength to strength.

Palmer's team had a good season with notable victories although his personal performances were something of a disappointment. In keeping with progress off the field the club entered the North Lancashire and District League for the 1901 season. In the seasons between 1901 and 1908 (the club withdrew for the 1905 season) a total of just five victories out of 70 games emphasized the step up in the class of cricket but in between the ten league games each year, the side where very successful against the local and visiting clubs. In August 1900 a Morecambe team undertook a successful tour to Ireland beating Strabane, Portrush, and Castlerock.

Throughout the early 1900's John Brooksbank continued to play excellent cricket and was rewarded in 1902 by being selected for the Eighteen of North Lancashire and District to play the Lancashire County at Lancaster on 2nd and 3rd of May. A strong Lancashire team scored 278 for 9 wickets with James Hallows scoring 101 and England international J.T. Tyldesley 51. Tyldesley went on to play 31 tests in total for England. Albert Hornby, George Littlewood, John Sharp, and Frank Hollins were other notable names in the Lancashire side. In reply the District scored 167 all out, Brooksbank making just three.

At the end of each league season the NLL champions would play a Rest of the League side. Brooksbank played in several of these games together with two other Morecambe players, Archie Sutcliffe and Ernest Flaxington.

At the AGM in March a new captain for the 1904 season was elected in Mr. WH Birch an ex Broughton Rangers footballer (Rugby League) he took over from the now Reverend Samuel Palmer. The committee informed the meeting that they were to resign from the Lancaster and District League due to the onerous regulations as to registration which caused difficulty in the selection of teams. In September 1903 the club held a major event to raise much-needed finance. A Musical Fete and Fancy Fair was held on the West End Pier throughout the week of September the 14th to the 19th. The club raised £405 to which the President Mr. Barnsbee said the Committee should be congratulated on its success. This enabled the club to start the following season debt-free. At the election of officers Mr. RGW Howson and Mr. F Bannister signaled their intent to resign from their positions of Hon Treasurer and Hon Secretary respectively. Mr. Howson had been associated with

North Lancashire and District *versus* Lancashire County.

Played at Lancaster, May 2nd and 3rd, **1902**.

LANCASHIRE COUNTY.

J. H. Stanning, c Rooke b Haines ...	11
A. Ward, b Mabbutt	25
J. T. Tyldesley, c Haines b Iddon ...	51
G. Potter, run out	0
— Hallows, c Linney b Purdy	101
F. H. Hollins, c Mabbutt b Haines...	57
A. H. Hornby, lbw b Haines	0
A. Eccles, c Collinge b Purdy	2
W. Cuttell, not out	8
J. Sharp, c Pennington b Haines ...	4
A. Thomas, not out...	8
G. Littlewood	
Extras	11
Total (for nine wickets)...	278

NORTH LANCASHIRE AND DISTRICT.

R. G. E. Mortimer, b Cuttell	1
J. W. Jackson, b Littlewood	12
F. W. Stileman, b Littlewood	0
Purdy, c Eccles b Sharp	32
F. Mabbutt, b Sharp	13
G. F. Linney, c Stanning b Sharp ...	27
A. R. Severn, b Sharp	0
E. F. Long, b Sharp	1
S. E. Osborne, st Thomas b Ward ...	11
E. Rooke, c Potter b Ward	13
R. W. Pennington, b Littlewood	8
— Taylor, st Thomas b Ward	8
J. Brooksbank, b Littlewood	3
J. Flaxington, lbw b Littlewood	1
W. G. Collinge, b Ward	1
A. C. Haines, b Ward	1
Iddon, not out	3
J. T. Sanderson, b Littlewood	15
Extras	17
Total	167

---

versus Rest of League.

Played at Lancaster, August 29th, 1903.

LANCASTER.

R. G. E. Mortimer, b Haines	5
E. Mortimer, c Bigg b Haines	3
J. T. Sanderson, c Jackson b Hordley	0
Iddon (pro.), c Hudson b Haines	15
J. Allen, junr., c Hudson b Brooksbank	16
A. R. Severn, c Long b Haines	11
T. W. Wells, c Bigg b Brooksbank ...	2
G. Warren, b Brooksbank	17
R. Hurtley, b Haines	0
E. T. Hannam, c Hudson b Brooksbank	10
J. Burtholme, not out	1
Extras	6
Total	86

REST OF LEAGUE.

G. S. Linney (Kendal), c Severn b Allen	14
J. W. Jackson (Ulverston), b Iddon ...	0
F. W. H. Stileman (Barrow), c Burtholme b Severn	50
G. A. Bigg, (Barrow), c and b Wells...	22
F. Mabbutt (Ulverston), run out	13
J. Brooksbank (Morecambe), lbw b Severn	9
E. Flaxington (Morecambe), not out...	11
E. F. Long, (Barrow), not out	7
Dr. Hudson (Millom)	
J. Hordley (Barrow)	
A. C. Haines, (Ulverston)	
Extras	10
Total (for six wickets)	136

the club for so long that he was regarded as the Father of the Club and had only resigned because of ill health. A vote of thanks was expressed for years of service and hard work to both men and further debate resulted in both being made Life Members.

The 1904 season was no different as Morecambe again finished at the foot of the NLL but a remarkable innings by John Brooksbank against Kendal on the Saturday of Whitsuntide weekend in May should be noted in that he scored a remarkable 132 out of a total of 176. No other Morecambe batsman managed to reach double figures. The scorecard is shown overleaf..

In 1907 John Brooksbank was elected captain and *'The Visitor'* gave a detailed account of this fine player. Brooksbank first played for a team connected with his church at Ilkley. He went on to play the Ilkley first team town club and as soon as he left Ilkley to move to Morecambe he joined the club. Playing for the club on the ground behind the old Midland Station in his first season he was the club's leading bowler and with the advent of boom times in Morecambe the club found a much greater supply of cricket talent he added. Seasons 1898-1900 were, he considered, the clubs most successful ones with stalwarts such as Weatherall, Makin, Palmer, Daniel, Schofield, McGregor, and McManus. Personally he recognised 1904 as his most successful season for not only scoring the magnificent 132 against Kendal he compiled a score of 138 against the Lancaster Grammar School. It was not unusual for schools to employ a professional at this time and Lancaster, together with Heversham and Sedbergh normally had a paid man in their ranks.

The *Lancaster Guardian* reported the match against the Grammar School as the following: *'The Lancaster Grammar School Eleven got badly cut up on their visit to Morecambe. The Seasiders' Brooksbank has probably never displayed more brilliant form with the bat, and he hit with remarkable freedom all around the wicket carrying his score to 138 before he was bowled by Deed.'*

Morecambe v Lancaster Grammar School		
Brooksbank	b.Deed	138
Healey	c.Taylor b.Deed	29
Flaxington	b.Deed	2
Bland	c.Barrow b.Deed	4
Sutcliffe	not out	11
Bibby	b.Deed	0
Slingsby	lbw Oglethorpe	6
	Extras	30
	For 6 wickets dec	220

Kendal		
Linney	c Watson b Brooksbank	126
Major	b Watson	24
Pepper (pro)	LBW Brooksbank	6
Pennington	Not Out	87
Hunter	Not Out	0
	Extras	9
	For 3 Wickets	252
Morecambe		
Brooksbank	b Pennington	132
Healey	Run Out	4
Barlow	b Pooley	0
Flaxington	c and b	4
Sutliffe	b Pooley	0
Hallam	b Pepper	7
Kitching	b Pennington	0
Hodgson	b Farrer	8
Watson	b Pooley	0
Wright	Not Out	6
Birch	b Pennington	4
	Extras	11
	All Out	176

Brooksbank was selected to play against the Lancashire County on two occasions but could not fulfill the first invitation due to business commitments and when asked about the present standard he remarked cricket was not good with a lack of interest among the young in the town. In Yorkshire every church or chapel has a club and this proved to be a nursery for young players, he added.

Such was Brooksbank's performances and dedication that in February 1910 a special gathering was held at the Pier Hotel for a presentation in celebration of 18 years' service to the club.

Prior to the presentation a supper was taken provided by the landlord Mr. F Troop, after which Mr. Smith presided and explained the gathering followed by a request for Mr. Dance to make the presentation. A fund had been put together with contributions from club members, businessmen within the town and some of opposition clubs who the club played on regular basis. From this fund Mr. Dance added that: *There is no doubt that if Mr. Brooksbank had considered his own financial standpoint he could have gained out of cricket he would have left long ago. He had paid his own expenses year after year without any remuneration and it was a great pleasure to make such a presentation to a great sportsman'.*

Brooksbank was then presented with a gold watch and a purse of gold. The watch bore the following inscription: 'Presented to Mr. J Brooksbank as a token appreciation from his many admirers in recognition of his 18 years' faithful service to MCC.' In response Brooksbank thanked all that had taken part in gathering the money. The gift was unexpected and he would value it more than anything in his possession. Brooksbank continued to play up until the outbreak of war in 1914.

A new captain in 1905 was Tom Kitching with Mr. HJ Jenkinson vice-captain. The club left the North Lancashire League for this season due to the high cost of travel together with the debt of the new pavilion still not settled. A return back to the league in 1906 culminated in the following year a severe financial crisis with the club's debt now at £1,225. The club's answer to write-off this debt was to hold 'a big bazaar'. How much income this realized over the Bank Holiday weekend we do not know but one report quoted the club had taken a £104 profit from the first day.

1909 was to be the club's last season in the North Lancashire & District League before the outbreak of war. The club continued to play a full fixture list but was in desperate need of support. An article on May 1st that year stressed it was only through the efforts of Secretary Kitching that the club was still in existence.

On the playing side dropping out of the league allowed John Brooksbank to take 92 wickets at an average of 7.69 each. Showing he could still bat he scored 412 runs at an average of 21.68 per innings. Of the 92 victims, 67 were bowled and eight LBW.
Morecambe seconds rejoined the Lancaster & District League for just one season in 1911 to continue the club's league membership merry-go-round.

In 1914 the club played a full fixture list and matches against Manchester Wanderers and Liverpool Tourists which created interest in the town. The Liverpool Tourists included the two Sugg brothers. Although well past their first class playing days they both performed admirably in the game. Frank Sugg had played two Tests for England, and 306 first-class games for Yorkshire, Lancashire and Derbyshire. His brother Walter played 129 games for Yorkshire and Derbyshire.

In August 1914 the local press reported details about the first battles of the war and an enlisting campaign to sign up one thousand men took place in the town. As a consequence the club's last game in 1914 was on August 15th against Holme. This resulted in victory by 117 to 34. These

Morecambe Cricket Club 1910.
Left to Right Standing- W. Mayor (Secretary)), Dr J.C.Ashton, R.Parker, W.E.Farrar, J. Brooksbank, Ald J.Snowden, J.Blades(scorer), J.Roscoe(umpire), Middle Row – W.J. Dance, T.Kitching, F.Bland(Capt), N.Morris, A.Sutcliffe, Front-The Rev D.R. Davies, H.Harland, A.Barnes.

were the names of that last team to play before Woodhill Lane was to lay dormant for the duration of World War One: F Bland, W Denbigh, R Howson, B Knowles, G Birkett, VJ Willis, J Parkinson, WJ Dance, C Simpson, J Carter and A Gibson.

It was inevitable that the conflict of war would claim the lives of men either currently or previously associated with the club. From the limited records available three such deaths should be recorded. In June 1917 Thomas Brockbank who lived at Nelson Street in the resort died from wounds received at Ypres. Educated at Lancaster Royal Grammar School he had initially worked for the Liverpool Bank at the Ambleside Branch before transferring in 1911 to Lancaster. He was a member of both the town's cricket and hockey clubs.

A village the size of Bare had few men eligible to enlist but John James

Parkinson was one who did and paid the ultimate sacrifice in July 1918. Prior to enlisting he worked at the Goods Yard at the Midland Station and was a former member of the club.

A third man who lost his life was Arthur Widdop educated at Lancaster Royal Grammar School he played cricket for Morecambe and Ulverston as well as rugby for Ulverston and the Vale of Lune. Prior to the war he had played for the Lancashire Rugby team and was employed as a clerk with the Lancaster Banking Company at Ulverston.

Chapter Two — The First Silverware

It was 1920 and the club looked to re-establish itself by taking up membership of the Lancaster & District League. The season opened in fine style with three straight wins against Williamsons, Storeys, and Lancaster 2nd X1. This resulted in them being regarded as favourites for the league. In June they went to Bentham and unaccountably lost by three runs. After a week went by with no cricket due to adverse weather they again lost, this time on home ground. A more determined effort was called for and victory against Low Bentham who were bowled out for 17 and 22 in consecutive weeks preceded two more victories to take them to the top of the league. With Heysham to play twice the Championship was considered as good as won.

The first of the derby games proved a thriller with Heysham winning by one run. Morecambe protested that the Heysham ground had been in bad condition and that any skillful cricket was nigh impossible. In the return match it was Heysham's turn to lose by a margin of five wickets.

That left the deciding game of the season against Storeys in what was regarded as a final. The winners of the match would automatically become champions. Morecambe were actually slightly better off as a draw would leave them a point ahead of their rivals. Storeys batted first and totaled 90, one of the highest scores of the season. Morecambe never looking like reaching the score and when captain Bland arrived at the wicket the Priory clock was striking six, he duly claimed a draw. Normally play should have ceased at that hour but for some unknown reason it was decided to carry on to seven o'clock. The game would probably have still ended in a draw had one umpire not given two highly debatable LBW decisions. Morecambe protested strongly but to no avail. A press note on the meeting read: *'The protest was disallowed but the chairman agreed that the umpiring was shocking.'*

A report some eight years later details the title being shared with Storeys. Which is true, we do not know but that was to be the last experience of the Lancaster and District League for the first team as they rejoined the North Lancashire & District League for the 1921 season.

Morecambe Football Club had agreed with the club to use the field for the 1920-21 season and on the 28th August 1920 the football club played host to Fleetwood in the opening game before a crowd of 3,000. The Football Club had applied to join the Lancashire Combination with the intention of playing in the second division, however they were allocated a place in the first division and much debate ensued as to if the local talent was up to the standard of the competition. For the record the football club lost that inaugural match 1-4 with Parker scoring for Morecambe.

Some of the attendances to the league games were sizeable. Against Barrow in December 1,600 people are recorded as watching the game. In early October, away at the Giant Axe in Lancaster, 3500 attended and a visit to league leaders Eccles United in November had 6,000 watching. With the ground in such poor condition at the end of the winter this was to be the football club's one and only season at Woodhill Lane. During that first season the football club also played its first FA Cup game against Breightmet United, a Bolton and District side, on the 25th September 1920 drawing 1-1. The following Wednesday afternoon a poor performance resulted in a 0-2 defeat in the replay.

During the War a Sports Club from the huge White Lund ammunition filling factory used the club for outdoor activities and reported in 1920 that they could not carry on. They asked if the Cricket Club could start again. A public meeting was held where it was understood the ground was held in trust for the club and the club was revived as the 'Morecambe Cricket and Athletic Club'. In the previous year the ground had been used by children from the grammar school under certain terms and conditions and during a casual meeting between officials of the club and the headmaster he remarked that he understood the Education Authority were interested in the purchase of the field for the school.

When the club's solicitor spoke with the County Education Authority, however, a contract was found to have been signed by the trustees. The club suddenly found that the ground was not now theirs and while the ground was being used by the White Lund Factory the trustees were having to fund the mortgage costing them several hundred pounds. The land could only be sold for games and sport and the headmaster Rev WH Counsell said: 'it was quite clear the club could not carry on with the mortgage as well as its other expenses'. Maybe the club would not have been able to carry on but the way the actions of the sale were conducted left much to be desired. The club would now be leasing the ground from the Education Authority as it would now be its landlord and the club the tenant. The ensuing years were to create a difficult relationship between the two organisations.

Fred Bland was again captain for the 1921 season. First game on returning to the NLL resulted in victory against Ulverston, but this was a poor season and it came as no surprise that at the club's AGM they again withdrew from the league. The standard of play was generally high and combined with the additional difficulty in arranging transport for such long journeys were the main contributors to this decision. The club's second and third teams were holding their own in the Lancaster and District League but it would be considered a backward step to put the first eleven back into that league. As a result the club were successful in applying for membership of the 'Palace Shield' a league which had teams from mainly the Preston and Fylde area of the county. It was considered there would be a reasonable chance of honours. This belief was speedily derailed as the club lost the first three games. Against St Annes they were all out for 23 although it must be said the opposition faired little better in making only 35. On the 20th May they achieved their first victory thanks to a newcomer Jimmy Thornton who made 60 runs in record time. Ervin Knight was another newcomer who came on the scene and mainly due to his efforts the team rose nearly half way up the league. It was a disappointing season after dropping into a lower league. The club's already serious financial position had got worse due to a constantly wet summer which reduced the 'gates' and a membership reduced by half.

Jimmy Thornton was promoted to captain in 1924 and a disastrous start as one point was taken from the first eight matches. Star batsman in this season was John Kitchen who had allowed himself to leave his beloved Heysham. At the end of July an outstanding batsman joined the club. He was Willie Wilkinson or known to his friends as Billy. A Yorkshireman he originally played for the Mount of Olive club in the Bradford League but he had achieved most success in the thirteen years he played at the Great Horton club. As captain he led the club to the double in 1909 winning the League Championship and the Priestley Cup.

Wilkinson had played with and against some of the best Yorkshire cricketers. At Great Horton he regularly opened the batting with Percy Holmes before Holmes went on to play for Yorkshire and England. His first game for Morecambe was in a friendly against Windermere scoring 85. After being eagerly pursued to play regularly by club officials, he soon excelled. In the same year at the close of the football season another distinguished newcomer joined the ranks in John Thompson, who had been professional at both Carnforth and Barrow.

Thompson took time to settle in but returned 8-10 against Great Eccleston as the club rose to finish fifth from the bottom after the poor

Morecambe Cricket Club First X1 1924
Standing –T. Hartley (Treasurer), W. Simpson, J. Carter, L. Noble, --------,
E. Hargreaves, J. Hargreaves (Secretary)
Seated J. Richardson, W.H. Wilkinson, Fred Bland, J.Thornton, T. B.
Hustler, ?.Green,
Front Scorer E.Wade. Two boys at the front are Fred Bland's sons -
Standing Bill Bland snr and Kneeling Arthur Bland

start. John Thompson was a goalkeeper who is credited with 32 league (six cup) appearances for Morecambe FC. Formerly with Southport he played for Barrow in their first ever Football League game against Stockport County on August 27th 1921. In 1921 when Morecambe went to play at Barrow Thompson was professional and proceeded to score 44 in double-quick time. In the return fixture at Morecambe he clean bowled four of the home team for a modest 15 runs and reduced them to the meekest submission. Little thought then that the same man was to play a prominent part in both the town's football and cricket clubs development. Tall and well built he could bowl as quickly as anyone in the NLL while his batting contributed in the middle order.

Prospects for the 1926 season were reported as being excellent as the clubs committee have been able to gather a strong team. The first eleven again entered the Palace Shield and the side were to be captained by Mr. WH Wilkinson. Conflicting reports say Wilkinson followed Fred Bland who resigned the captaincy after many years and not Jimmy Thornton. Fred Bland is recorded as playing his first games for the club in the late 1890's. His father Mr. Thomas Bland played for the club at the original Summer Gardens ground.

This was the last year for the first eleven in the Palace Shield. They finished in third place and but for three drawn games all of which saw Morecambe in a strong position they might have been on equal terms with the leaders.

If the Palace Shield was not as high a standard of cricket as the NLL then it was certainly as competitive as the following account from 'The Morecambe Guardian' shows with regard to a game against St Annes:

'Both teams were strong contenders for the championship. The visitors made 163 for eight wickets whereupon there position was considered impregnable to warrant a declaration, especially as only an hour and a half remained for play. They had reckoned without Wilkinson who found the bowling exactly to his taste. No one could stay with him more than a few minutes but so long as the score mounted rapidly wickets were of secondary importance.

' The last twenty minutes were a travesty of cricket. St Annes tried every conceivable means of time wasting. They called for sawdust, though it was a perfectly dry wicket, they set and reset the field, they changed bowlers more for the sake of passing time than in hope of disposing of Wilkinson. The last over began with Morecambe needing two to win with four wickets to fall. Hunt made the scores level and then Wilkinson was out. Immediately the fielders trooped to the pavilion refusing to complete the over because time was up. Perhaps it was; they saved a point but at the cost of their reputation.'

Prior to the start of the 1927 season the club received a generous gift of sightscreens from the president Mr. JB Christie. *'The Morecambe Guardian'* added: *'They will be a great asset to batsman who have in the past been troubled with passing trains and a dark background at the town end. Another innovation is an enclosure for deckchairs so that spectators will be made thoroughly comfortable.'*

The club rejoined the North Lancashire League and the 2nd XI left the Lancaster and District League to play in the Palace Shield. The 3rd XI would continue in the district league and play at the home of Morecambe Football Club, Christie Park.

Fixtures in the North Lancashire League were disjointed in that all clubs tended to play a different amount of games. Whitehaven, no doubt due to their geographic isolation, regularly only managed to play just twelve games during the 1920's while Dalton always seemed to play twenty two games. Being the new boys and looking at past history everybody wanted to play Morecambe, if not for the cricket and a potential victory then certainly a night out in this expanding waterfront town.

Putting aside the club's previous form in this league it immediately found a measure of success by reaching the Higson Cup Final. These matches were played on midweek evenings with no limitations. This resulted in some games being played over two, three, or even four nights until a conclusion was reached. The Higson Cup was geographically zoned in the first round to cut down on travel for both players and supporters.

Another consequence of the 'timeless ties' were high scores and in 1924 Millom scored a record 414-7 declared against Vickerstown. Kendal-based Netherfield, or the K Shoes works team as they were known, were admitted to the league in 1926 and in the first round of the 1927 Higson Cup were drawn away to Morecambe. Batting first Netherfield made 152. Morecambe played strongly and surpassed their total to win by 8 wickets with WH (Billy) Wilkinson scoring 111. In a second round game against Kendal victory was achieved by the huge margin of 253 runs. Once again gain Wilkinson was the hero scoring a century with a magnificent 119 in a total of 326 racked up by the home team. Kendal could only muster 73 as Len Noble helped himself to six wickets.

This brought a semi-final against Dalton played on a Wednesday evening. Dalton batted first and made 113 with John Thompson taking 4-37. Morecambe's reply of 116-3 included a knock of 73 not out from Wilkinson. Wilkinson's efforts were recognised by selection to the League side to play the Cumberland county side in the annual fixture.

The final against Furness was played at Barrow's Monks Croft ground. Finals were held on a Sunday with gate receipts going into league funds. At the end of the season this ground was to be renamed the Ernest Pass Memorial Ground in memory of the son of the Barrow chairman Alfred Pass who had been killed in the Great War.

Morecambe entered the game as favourites and seemed to justify this billing when Furness made just 121. A cautious reply took the seasiders to 60 for the loss of three wickets. At this point the *Morecambe Guardian* reported: *'The game slowed down and the fastest moving*

```
Higson Cup 2nd Round 25th June 1927

Morecambe
WH Wilkinson          Run Out                          119
F Bland               c. Wildman.b.Hall                 16
J Thompson            b. Hall                           23
L Noble               LBW  Hall                          0
JS Crowther           b. Low                            47
T Hunt                LBW Pennington                    13
T Hustler             b. Dawson                         18
R Simpson             b. Hall                            7
JR Richardson         b. Hall                           29
F Naylor              Not Out                           16
A Barnes              b. Hall                           11
                                        Extras          27
                                        Total          326
Kendal
G Wileman             b.Noble                            7
J Heap                c.Richardsonb.Noble               1
TD Page               b.Noble                            3
T Pooley              c.Simpson.b.Thompson              15
G Thackeray           b.Noble                            4
Hall(pro)             b.Noble                            0
FC Worth              c.Richardson.b.Noble              5
WF Pennington         b.Thompson                         1
T Low                 Not Out                           13
RB Dawson             c.Richardson.b.Thompson           18
                                        Extras           6
                                        Total           73
```

object on the ground was a member of the Morecambe committee running to telephone his team's happy position.'

When Foley departed for 25 he was to be followed by a collapse that saw Morecambe all out for 106 and defeat by just 15 runs. Foley had previously played for the Preston club and a couple of games for Lancashire second eleven in the Minor Counties Championship prior to the First World War.

At the conclusion of the match Mr. TA Higson, the donor of the cup presented it to F Mercer captain of the winning Furness team. He went on to congratulate Morecambe on their good performance on re-entering the league.

The following Saturday a league fixture against Furness was played and to the frustration of the members victory by 39 runs was achieved, Morecambe making 91 and Furness 52. John Thompson took 6-21 and as the curtain came down on the season Thompson had taken 105 wickets, 98 in the North Lancashire League and seven in the Palace Shield. A final position of third place was a major achievement after the dismal times of Palace Shield cricket but there was better to come.

Starting the 1928 season with much the same team, the press made Morecambe favourites for the league title. An opening defeat against Millom must have focused the team as they than proceeded to climb the league table. A notable individual bowling performance of 8-10 from Jimmy Carter in victory over Carnforth led Morecambe on their way to the top of the league. Further recognition for the club came as both Thompson and Wilkinson were selected for the league side to play the Cumberland County in the annual fixture at Millom on June 20th.

After victory against Vickerstown at the end of July the team looked certain league champions but the following week a defeat against Netherfield by one wicket only served to show that no side could be taken lightly. In this game John Thompson took 9-39 and rumours were that he was being lined up for a 'pro' job in the Ribblesdale League. Wins against Vickerstown (again) and South Ulverston over the August Bank Holiday kept the side at the top, Wilkinson hitting 101 not out in the South Ulverston victory by seven wickets.

Three games were left; Barrow their nearest challengers home and away sandwiched by Dalton. Victory in the first game against Barrow would have secured the title but defeat meant the same scenario against Dalton. Again the team froze and a dour draw was played out by Morecambe. Morecambe's last game was against Barrow and a disastrous defeat, losing by three wickets meant if Barrow won their last game a play-off would be required. Against Kendal the Barrovians were defeated by 110 runs and Morecambe were named champions for 1928.

At the end of September the President Mr. JB Christie presented the league trophy to captain Fred Bland at a supper held at the Imperial Hotel. Mr. Christie then presented gold medals to members of the team. Mr. Bland replied by thanking Mr. Christie for his generosity and added that although Morecambe could not afford a professional John Thompson was as good as any pro in the league. He then handed a leather cricket bag as a personal gift to Thompson. Thompson had taken 72 wickets at 9.25 runs apiece and Wilkinson had scored 553 runs. Mr. Bland related to his years of playing for Morecambe in that he said: "*There was only one captain's name on the cup since 1892 he had not played against.*" Willie Wilkinson then handed Mr. Bland a mounted cricket ball as a token of regard from the players to which Mr.

Bland suitably acknowledged the gift and added he was proud to have captained a North Lancashire League championship winning team.

At the AGM it was reported that not only had the 1st XI had success the 2nd XI had finished third in The Palace Shield and the 3rd XI had also finished third in the Lancaster & District League. This success had only brought about a profit of £4 6s 4d on the season and once again the townspeople were asked to support the club. Mr. JR Richardson proposed Mr. Fred Bland as a Life Member and this was followed by Mr. GH Varley who proposed Mr. Tom Kitching as a Life Member. Both propositions were carried.

In 1921 in a match between the Morecambe Wednesday and Sefton College teams, a youth of large proportions scored the majority of the College's runs and then took six wickets at a low cost. That youth was Tom Hustler, who joined the club immediately afterwards. In his first game he all but made the top score before temporarily disappearing from the scene. The returning Tom Hustler was a prominent player having played in both the 1927 Higson Cup final and the Championship winning team of 1928. For the 1929 season Hustler was to be captain.

There was another youngster whose performances in the second team attracted considerable attention in that same year of 1921. That was Tommy Hunt who gave sterling service to the club as a player and administrator.

One of Hustler's first duties prior to the start of the season was to present a clock on behalf of the Grammar school and Cricket club to Frank Jubb who was leaving the area to become Head Groundsman at Sedbergh School. Jubb came to Morecambe in 1920 and remarked on how when he arrived the club had trouble raising two sides but things were a lot healthier now as the club proposed to run four sides in the forthcoming season. Jubb was a member of a well known Yorkshire farming family and fine amateur horseman. He rode in Point-to-Point Steeplechases with success at local meetings and was also a keen Rugby Union player. He served the Sedbergh School for 14 years before his sudden death while on holiday in Morecambe in late September 1942.

The 1929 season opened with John Thompson not playing and more concerning not replaced. Two drawn games were followed by a heavy defeat against Dalton and this set the precedent for an average season and mid table finish.

Playing four teams each week proved to be a struggle. This new initiative was abandoned after the one season but a report in the *'Morecambe Guardian'* added: *'Morecambe have a promising batsman in Foster, 12 years of age he is a pupil at West End Council School, has a fine defence and playing for the fourth eleven has given every indication of becoming a fine batsman.'* Foster was to go on and hold a regular first team place as opening bat.

1929 saw the club mourn the death of its President Mr. Joseph Barnes Christie at his residence 'Queensholme' Mayfield Drive, Morecambe.
76 years of age and a native of Accrington he was for many years in business as a member of the firm of Messrs Myrtle, Burt and Co, exporters and merchants, of Manchester, who dealt mainly in trade from the Dutch East Indies. He had lived in Morecambe for ten years and was a generous benefactor to many organizations in the town.

After Morecambe Football Club's enforced move from Woodhill Lane after the 1920-21 season Mr. Christie donated the land at Roseberry Park/Lancaster Road to the club. The football ground was then named after him as Christie Park. The funeral took place at Duke Street Cemetery, Southport with a service being held at St Laurence Church, Morecambe prior to the internment. Amongst the many floral tributes at the funeral the Cricket Club sent a model of a cricket pitch represented by flowers. Representatives of the club in attendance were Messrs F Bland, EA Varley, WH Hirst and JS Robinson.

Chapter Three — Beer and Skittles

After the euphoria of winning the championship in 1928 the club declined with average performances on the field. In 1929 and 1930 the club finished fourth from the bottom on both occasions and in an attempt to bring more supporters down the Lane, the Public Parks and Pleasure Grounds Committee of the local Borough agreed to an application from the club to use boards on the promenade (these were also used by the football club in winter) during the summer to advertise the forthcoming matches.

One of the reasons for the poor performances was the absence of John Thompson who had emigrated to Canada after the season of 1928. Thompson was back for the 1931 season and duly made captain of a young side. The local press criticized the side's indifferent performances and the captain told them to be patient. Thompson himself was selected for the League team to play the Ribblesdale League and due mainly to his performances the side finished in a credible equal-fourth place with Whitehaven and Millom.

At the North Lancashire League AGM in January an application had been received to join the Senior League by Cumberland Motor Services. This was a team based in Whitehaven but they gave assurances to the league they would play matches at Cleator and run a bus from Millom station for the Furness clubs to the Cleator ground. Their application was accepted but not without the Morecambe and Carnforth clubs giving grave concerns about travel time and expense. In the end CMS played at Whitehaven and the concerns voiced were fully vindicated.

Tommy Hunt was elected captain for the 1932 season and a call was made for players of cricket within the town to join the club as a shortage was envisaged. The opening game resulted in an unexpected victory against Dalton. Dalton had been unbeaten for the last two years on their ground and could only manage 94 all out as Morecambe replied with 96-5, Matt Forrest scoring 35 not out and Percy Sissons taking 5-30.

To his credit Hunt led from the front as the club finished a creditable fifth with six wins twelve defeats and three draws in twenty one league and cup games. Hunt was leading run scorer with 330 followed by Carter with 323. Frank Naylor had the highest score of the season when making 55. Morton took 18 wickets for 85 runs before getting injured and Sissons showed promise in his first season taking 26 wickets at 13.3 runs.

At the AGM a disappointing loss of £36 on the season was recorded. Contributing factors were a £5 decrease in subscriptions, £37 down on socials, and catering profit down £16.

1933 saw the club revert back to engaging a professional. Secured for the season was ex-Sussex player Don Jenner or to give him his full name Felix Donovan Jenner. Jenner was a tall man, his speciality being the straight drive. The Sussex and England legend Maurice Tate was opening the bowling and taking 150 wickets a season for the county and as a result Jenner was seldom called upon to bowl for Sussex. Having been professional for Lancaster in the Ribblesdale League in seasons 1925 to 1927 Jenner excelled with the bat before accepting an offer to play for Leyland Motors. Indifferent professionals engaged by Lancaster resulted in them bringing the Sussex man back to Lune Road for a further three seasons, 1930 to 1932. Now at 40 years of age he was to take up the 'paid' job at Woodhill Lane.

In the opening game Jenner took 3-28 with the ball and scored 11 with the bat as Morecambe slipped to defeat away at Furness. Jenner played a further four games before being struck with illness and his contract was mutually terminated. A poor season ensued emphasizing the need for a professional. The club had a debt of £65 and at an Extraordinary Annual General Meeting at the Ambulance Hall on the 7th September 1933 Mr. Walter Bell gave an overview of increased traveling expenses, poor support for socials, and groundsman's fees suggesting the following remedial action: 1 More intensive patrons list; 2 The Mayor to open a subscription list; 3 A sale of work; 4 The club to withdraw the second team from the Palace Shield into the Lancaster and District League to reduce traveling and umpires fees.

Mr. Bell's rallying call must have worked as prior to the following season the club was free from debt due to as 'The Visitor' quoted: 'the efforts of loyal supporters over the winter months'.

Mr. Tommy Hunt was re-elected captain for the 1934 season and then it was announced that Syd Youren would play for the club after taking over the Devonshire Billiard Hall and moving to reside at Heysham.

For the 1934 season a new professional JE Brierley who hailed from Haslingden was appointed. Brierley had played with Queensbury in the Bradford League the season previous and immediately made an impression in the opening game taking 3-40 and scoring 46 in the victory over Vickerstown. The side continued to produce excellent results with one of the highlights being a hat-trick by Percy Sissons against Furness.

At the start of June the side was at the top of the table but in the game against Netherfield an unprecedented incident resulted in a decline of form. Playing against Netherfield at Parkside Road John Thompson had opened the bowling taking the early wickets of Noble and King. Thompson was bowling well enough but WH Davies the former Glamorgan player and now the Netherfield professional was taking a liking to the bowling as the score steadily progressed. Hunt the Morecambe captain replaced Thompson with Naylor who bowled tight but took no wickets. Thompson was then called back into the attack but in his first over three boundaries were scored. Hunt subsequently made another change. Later in the innings Hunt asked Thompson to bowl again. At this point words were exchanged and Thompson was left in no doubt that he was required to bowl or leave the field. Thompson took the later option as he refused to bowl. The game continued and Netherfield finished their innings with a total of 155. In reply a disjointed Morecambe could only score 41 with the word 'absent' against Thompson's name on the scorecard, Davies the opposition professional taking 7-22.

The following week a hastily arranged committee meeting discussed the issue and chairman Walter Bell made a statement to the effect that although Thompson was one of the best players in the league, the committee supported the captain and Thompson must apologise for his actions. If he did so added Mr. Bell then the matter would be closed, if not the committee would take whatever action they deemed appropriate. No apology was received and Thompson was not selected for the following week's game against Carnforth. Thompson wrote to the *Morecambe Guardian* to put forward his case but no resolution was found and in early August it was rumored Thompson was to play for Heysham in the Westmorland League.

Needless to say the following week the side lost to Carnforth and as with any side missing its strike bowler the sides performances faltered to leave them finishing in sixth place. Despite the internal wrangling Syd Youren in his first season at the club was the league's highest aggregate run scorer although the league's average winner was Chadwick from Whitehaven. Youren's highlight of the season was making an undefeated 101 away at Ulverston.

Syd Youren was a North Lancashire League legend whose run scoring feats were at that time unsurpassed. Youren was a professional in all but the fact the player never played first-class cricket. An all round sportsman he played football for Barrow in their Lancashire Combination side and also played Rugby League for Millom. Moving from club to club wherever a contract was offered his batting is still unique today from the records we have available. From 1922 to 1939 Youren finished in the top ten of the league's averages on sixteen occasions. He had the highest aggregate in six of these years and he also won the averages outright in four of these years. He scored the most runs in consecutive years from 1923 to 1927. In 1923 as professional at Vickerstown he scored almost 800 runs to create a new league batting record. Youren was also professional at Millom, Dalton, Whitehaven and Haverigg. In 1923 he played three games for Lancashire 2nds with little success but in 1926 his run scoring was recognised as his name was included in a Cumberland squad of seventeen players to play the touring Australians in a one day game.

This squad included such legends as Patsy Hendren, Herbert Sutcliffe, George Gunn and Roy Kilner. As a result it was no surprise that Youren was left out and only one Cumberland player represented the

Syd Youren

Confirmation of Youren's selection for the Cumberland side to play the 1927 touring New Zealanders

county that being Roland Saint. The pinnacle of his career was in 1927 when he played for the Cumberland county team against the touring New Zealanders at Whitehaven in a two day game. Batting first Youren top scored with 44 from a Cumberland total of 154. The tourists then scored 302 followed by a reply of 130 by the home side of which Youren made 19. Youren made other appearances for the Cumberland County and the representative League side. Although 1934 was his last season for either topping league 'averages or aggregates' his vast experience was to transform the team over the next few seasons.

THE LANCASHIRE COUNTY
AND MANCHESTER CRICKET CLUB.

26, Barton Arcade,
Manchester.

Dear Sir,   15th, June, 1923.

You have been selected to play for Lancashire
2nd against Durham at Chester le Street on Monday and
Tuesday, June 25 & 26, 1923 also against Northumberland at
Jesmond on June 27 & 28.

The team will travel by the 2 p.m train from
Victoria Station Manchester, on Sunday June 24th.

Rooms have been reserved at The County Hotel,
Newcastle on Tyne.

The team will meet at the Victoria Station
Booking Office, Manchester, on Sunday June 24th at 1-45
p.m and Mr J. T. Tyldesley will obtain the Railway tickets.

Please confirm by return of post.

Yours Faithfully,

H. Rylance
Secretary.

Invitation to join the Lancashire 2nd's team playing at Jesmond

Youren's performances were well reported in various local newspapers around North Lancashire and one article from *'The Visitor'* contained the following reference to his arrival into the Morecambe side:

'Not for some years has Morecambe cricket been as solid as it is today, but it has had brighter and more vivid eras .Although today it is a reliable run-making machine with as many of crickets uncertainties eliminated as it is possible to eliminate, it had more general colour in the time of Counsell ,Thornton and Wilkinson.

'But in those big-hitting days there was no Youren and I suppose it's safe

to say that never has Morecambe had such a batsman as he is (in fact has the North Lancashire League ?. When he makes his slow walk from the pavilion to the wicket something of a hush falls on the spectators as through a reverence. A bad start does not always mean a short innings as some of his best scores have been made after a shaky start. But whether ten, fifty, or a hundred Youren is a personality with little mannerisms that go with it. His habits of twisting his bat in his hand before receiving the ball and his glance up to the sky as he walks from the wicket after being out never leave him.

' I often wonder what this looking to the sky heavenwards means is it a call to a higher witness that Youren was not out or agreement that he was ?

' In the Higson Cup match against Netherfield I saw him swivel like lightening and hook a ball chin high past fine leg for four. Davies was the bowler and one of the fastest. North Lancashire League batsman twenty years younger than Youren would not attempt this shot without the risk of a broken jaw or the loss of front teeth'.

The article finished with a fitting tribute.

'When Youren retires much of the light will go not only from Morecambe cricket but from the North Lancashire League.'

The Annual Dinner held in March the following year had as its guest Councillor A Gorton who when addressing the audience remembered the dinner of 1903 he attended from which the inception of the Morecambe Debating Society was formed. Adding he wished that these things should be remembered. Councilor Gorton then reminded club members that it was he who had had the unpleasant task of purchasing the ground for the Grammar School but then said that the club could probably buy back the ground in two to three years if they could outbid the Council. As it was, that opportunity never came to fruition.

Mr. Walter Bell spoke to members suggesting that a national competition for clubs similar to the Football Association Cup should be introduced and that Morecambe should take the lead by arranging a conference for all the leagues to be held in the resort so that the details could be drawn up. This did not happen of course until the introduction of the National Knock- Out competition many years later but Mr. Bell was certainly in front of the time with his suggestion.

In 1935 Noel Rhodes was engaged as the club professional and Syd

Youren took over as captain. Rhodes had been professional at Walsden in the Central Lancashire League for the previous three years and in 1929 he made two appearances for Lancashire 2nds. Another new face that season was a former Ramsbottom professional and ex-member of the Surrey groundstaff, one Ed Moxham or to give him his full name, Edward Theodore Springett Moxham. With the 2nd team always starting a week earlier in the Palace Shield Competition Moxham was given a game as he had been out of the game for three years. The following week was the opening first team fixture and defeat to Ulverston. Playing Ulverston again in back to back fixtures Moxham opened the bowling with professional Rhodes each taking 5 wickets to bowl out the opposition for 77.

John Thompson was back in the fold, apology or not we may never know, but was missing in June and most of July with an ankle injury and although he returned at the end of July his injury restricted the amount of overs he could bowl. The highlight of the season was the August Bank Holiday weekend when Noel Rhodes became the first Morecambe player to take all ten wickets in a competitive league game. although Archie Sutcliffe had taken 10-9 against Horton Dyeworks on the last weekend of the 1904 season. In the Monday fixture against Millom, Syd Youren helped himself to 104 in the victorious total of 227-8 followed by Rhodes taking 6-31 in Millom's 91 all out. A strong run in to the end of the season saw the side finish mid-table.

Prior to the conclusion of the season club chairman Walter Bell

Furness				Morecambe		
JN Hexham	b.Rhodes		8	H Foster	b.Tallon	8
RA Banks	b.Rhodes		23	P Sisson	b.Sneesby	20
RC Houston	c.Hunt.b.Rhodes		4	WM Forrest	c.Fallowfield.b.Tallon	21
HC Butterworth	c.Dean.b.Rhodes		0	R Dean	LBW.Tallon	20
W Fallowfield	b.Rhodes		8	F Naylor	c.Paterson.b.Hewitson	0
T Keightley	c.Foster.b.Rhodes		2	J Thompson	c.Mitchell.b.Hewitson	10
W Hewitson	b.Rhodes		0	N Rhodes	c.Fallowfield.b.Tallon	0
L Mitchell	b.Rhodes		28	A Hartley	Not Out	7
A Paterson	c.Foster.b.Rhodes		3	T Hunt	LBW.Hewitson	4
H Tallon	b.Rhodes		4		Extras	5
KR Sneesby	Not Out		0		Total for 8 wkts	95
		Extras	6			
		Total	86			
Bowling						
J Rhodes	19.5	9	28	10		
J Thompson	16	2	33	0		
W Simpson	8	3	19	0		

Noel Rhodes 10-wicket performance against Furness

announced finances and poor support would not allow the retention of Rhodes as the club professional. Rhodes performances certainly warranted him being resigned and Bell paid tribute to his performances when presenting him with the ball he took 10-28 against Furness. Rhodes thanked the club for the token which he would cherish in memory of a happy season at Morecambe and afterwards Captain Smith made a strong appeal for greater support from within the town for the town's club.

At the Annual General Meeting the members received a motion from the committee to disband. This was unanimously rejected. The proposition came about in a meeting where their was much straight talking about some of the players drinking on the journey to away games and allegations of objectionable language being used in the dressing room. It was emphasized that only a very small minority of first team players were to blame and it was added that the main offender was no longer associated with the club.

Mr. Walter Bell gave some background as to the reason to put forward the motion to disband. He said: *"it was only intended as a pious resolution to test the members and to bring the matter to a head"*

He added *"that things had been very unsatisfactory during the summer. The committee fully understood they could not carry on the club from gate money, but there had been deplorable apathy on the part of the members. They should understand that their obligations as members do not finish with paying a subscription of 12/6 and going down to the field on practice nights and Saturdays".*

To make traveling expenses easier for the players the committee had introduced a plan that regardless of playing at home or away players would contribute 1 shilling and 6 pence each instead of paying their fares for away matches in total which sometimes amounted to a large amount to pay at once. Mr. Bell added:

"Some of the players grumbled when the secretary approached them for the money and was met with discourtesy and an adjective. He was doing his work to help the club and should not be subjected to such abuse. There has not been a nice feeling in the team somehow. There has not been a nice cricket spirit. There's been a lot of grumbling. The resolution to wind up the club was put forward as the result of an aggregation of little pin-pricks".

Debate then centered around the issue of players drinking on the way to matches.

Mr. T Hartley said spectators at Vickerstown had noticed the effect of beer on certain Morecambe players. Mr. Horace Hutchence said players in the second and third teams had been reluctant to play in the first team the previous season because a habit had developed of stopping at Ulverston on the way home. The stop was too long and too late he added and the result was the team did not get back to Morecambe until about 11p.m.

The President Mr. Fred Bland said it would be deplorable if the club was allowed to go out of existence. The resolution to disband was withdrawn and it was unanimously decided to carry on.

The Chairman pointed out that a £30 credit balance last year had been turned into a deficit of £19 and they had to carry on more cheaply. One of the steps taken to save £20 a year was to move the club's second team to the Westmorland League for the 1936 season with the third team remaining in the Lancaster and District League. It was decided to form a ladies team to stimulate feminine interest in the club. It as also announced in direct contrast that the tennis section of the club had died a natural death as their courts could not compete with others in the town.

In March 1936 prior to the start of the season Mr. Walter Bell resigned from his post of chairman due to business reasons. At an EGM Captain A Smith a life member of the Nelson Cricket Club and a vice President of Colne Cricket Club was elected as Mr. Bell's successor. Mr. Smith was also the elected former MP for the Colne Division. From the meeting Mr. Bell was elected a life member, only the third person to hold the position.

Prior to the start of the season Mr. Fred Bland, the clubs president sent a letter to 'The Visitor' asking for support. The paper printed the letter in full and praised Mr. Bell for his efforts while asking for the towns sportsmen to support the club . He added: ' I have no fear that a good standard of cricket will be available and hope to thereby to see the championship flag flying again at Woodhill Lane.'

The opening fixture of 1936 resulted in victory against the previous season's champions Vickerstown, Morecambe making 71 to the opposition's 47, Percy Sissons taking 7-13. With regard to the advent of women's cricket a number of midweek games had been arranged to be played in the evenings with Miss I Willacy as captain. In early May came a victory over Barrow with the returning Tom Hustler from Lancaster scoring 56 with 11 boundaries. Making their first appearance for the club that day was Ray Ratten the Australian and the new professional Walker Ellis the ex- Lancashire player. Ellis had played for the Red Rose county between 1920 and 1923 making 36 appearances and scoring one century. After failing to secure a first team place Ellis was released by the county. In 1933 to 1934 he was professional at Carnforth and the previous season had been with Lancaster in the Ribblesdale League. Other appointments had been at Dunfermline were he had also played for Fifeshire, Blakeley in the Manchester Federation, Heaton in the Bolton League and Holmfirth in the Huddersfield League.

After defeating Carnforth in the first round of the Higson Cup a five wicket victory over Barrow in the return fixture at the end of May. Barrow made a total of 229-6 declared to which Morecambe replied with 234-5, Syd Youren scoring 72, Tom Hustler 43 and Walker Ellis taking 5-46. Barrow's professional that day was Billy Williams who made 115 not out and took four of the Morecambe wickets to fall. Further success ensued until a heavy defeat against Kendal. This was Ellis's benefit game and although Kendal were bowled out for 99,

Morecambe could only muster 28. Taking 3-26 off 15 overs Ellis then top scored with 15. The local press reported the largest crowd of the season and Ellis received a standing ovation when he was dismissed as

Walker Ellis, Lancashire CCC and
Morecambe Professional, 1936

if he had scored a century.

A victory against Millom on Bank Holiday Monday by one wicket with Frank Naylor scoring 52 kept the side in championship contention. Women's cricket was at the forefront again with a match between the ladies of Lancashire and Yorkshire on a Monday afternoon in August in front of a large crowd. As the run-in proceeded a defeat against Furness was followed by victories against Dalton and Haverigg, Ratten scoring 70 and Cross taking 6-8 to set up the last weekend of the season and a conclusion which was to be one of the most dramatic and controversial in the North Lancashire League's history. It should also be mentioned that the second team won the second division on the Westmorland League in their first season the previous Saturday.

Back then to those last fixtures of the 1936 season on the 12th September. All teams played the same number of games, though not against all of the clubs, the percentage system had been dropped. Morecambe were top of the league with 40 points, CMS and Netherfield were joint second with 39 points. Morecambe were playing Netherfield and although play started at 5.20 with play due to finish at 7.30 there was little chance of a result. In the end Morecambe made 85-4 and each side had to settle for one point each. CMS persuaded bottom of the league Lindal to play in the rain and by winning the game took three points and the championship. There were no 'phones in the clubhouse in 1936 unlike today's communications so Lindal would not have known the Netherfield/Morecambe game was destined for a draw with only two hours play. The Morecambe players were convinced that they had won the league until the news filtered through that CMS had played and won.

The following Saturday Morecambe seconds through winning the Second Division of the Westmorland League played the Division One winners who were Holme. Included in the Morecambe team was professional Walker Ellis but this could not prevent Holme winning with the scores being 111 to 96 all out.

Chapter Four — Team of 1937

After the disappointment of 1936 a new professional was announced, one Rennie Nutter. A traveled journeyman he was a medium fast bowler who had shown in previous professional engagements that he could bat as well. The credentials of Nutter could not be faulted and a resume of previous performances made him an attractive signing for the club. Although he had no first-class experience unlike his predecessor Walker Ellis it is difficult to understand how he was never given a chance at county level.

Nutter's career began in 1905 when he played for Colne in the Lancashire League. Two years later he left to play in Northern Ireland where he achieved the rare feat of a 'double hat-trick' and was then honoured as the first professional to play for the Ulster Province. Although that game resulted in defeat he justified his selection by taking all seven wickets of the opposition to fall. Returning to England in 1910 he joined Clitheroe were he topped the bowling averages. Moving on to Burnley St Andrews he was largely responsible for them winning the Ribblesdale League championship. In 1913 he returned to Colne as an amateur. Halfway through the season he headed the bowling averages along with Parkin and Llewellyn two of the country's most respected cricketers. This performance then earned him with another appointment with Crewe in the North Staffordshire League.

After the war Nutter returned to Colne as professional. He then began a long association with Formby, which saw him turn in some remarkable performances. Playing against New Brighton and joining his captain with four wickets down for 40 runs the pair added 197 runs in record time before being separated. Nutter's share was 99. In 1923 he scored 680 runs and captured 143 wickets. Two years later he achieved the even more remarkable performance of 1,080 runs and 114 wickets.

This happy association came to an end when he joined Milnrow in the Central Lancashire League for the 1927 season. His best performance in that season was 9-20 against Oldham.

Another club that benefited from his exceptional skill was New Brighton. On two occasions he took a 'hat-trick' and batting against Liverpool he was out four short of his century.

His next experience was with Old Hill in the Birmingham League. Through primarily a bowler he hit the Stourbridge bowling for a century in just 75 minutes. After another season with Colne he joined Bootle, but in 1935 he joined Liverpool Collegiate as a coach, a position he held with distinction.

For all his experience Nutter could not prevent defeat in the opening game of the season away against Netherfield in which Morecambe were all out for 29 in reply to the home team's 99. The following week Nutter showed his class with a home victory by six wickets against Dalton taking 9-23. Away at Ulverston the side encountered a rare tie with both sides scoring 70 runs apiece. A Higson Cup first round game and victory against Carnforth saw an Australian called Reg Ratten score 82 not out and pocket himself a collection of 39 shillings. A total of 153-6 was too many for Carnforth who replied with 113-9 before time was called. Since Morecambe and other sides had scored heavily in the Higson Cup the League had brought in a time limit of two hours 30 minutes for each innings. Press reports explained that Ratten would have gone on to score a century had time been allowed, but what this innings did show was that Morecambe had recruited another player of some repute. Ratten had played Grade cricket in Australia and Woodhill Lane must have seemed a long way from the heat of Melbourne.

A progression of games followed with resounding wins and in the league game away at Carnforth a new player appeared on the teamsheet. Opening the bowling with Nutter was one Ambrose Causer Williams (Billy). An ex-Yorkshire player he took 3-21 as Morecambe, dismissed for 105 bowled Carnforth out for 45, Nutter having the excellent figures of 13.1 overs, 5 maidens, 17 runs, 7 wickets. At the end of July an away game at Kendal had resulted in Morecambe hanging on for a draw with the match scores Kendal 162-7 and Morecambe 101-8, Williams taking 5-47 from 20 overs. The following week was the return fixture at Woodhill Lane. Morecambe were at full strength but Kendal were missing Coldham and Crawford, two Sedbergh schoolmasters who had gone south for two weeks. The biggest gate for many years realised takings of 11 pounds. An all round performance saw Morecambe win. Batting first they scored 115 with Williams scoring 38 and Foster 34. Kendal replied with 84 and Nutter took 6-26 from 16.2 overs.

In the away fixture at Barrow Rennie Nutter took his 100th wicket in all competitions as Morecambe won by seven wickets. The following week in the return fixture victory secured the league title as Morecambe scored 147, with Ratten 58 and Foster 43 the main contributors. Nutter was at his best as Barrow were all out for 50. Nutter's figures were 16.1 overs, 6 maidens, 19 runs, 8 wickets. A final win away to Haverigg capped off a victorious season for a side that were worthy North Lancashire League champions.

Morecambe were generally received as worthy champions but the *'Barrow News'* made the following post match comment: *'Just one word to Morecambe. I have rarely heard as many appeals during a short innings as the visiting side made. Actually one appeal was for LBW when the bat had glided the ball to the pavilion steps by the bat. Cut some of this out Morecambe !'*

Nutter's haul in league games was 102 wickets, the highest in the league and the average winner. A celebration dinner was held at The King's Arms and chairman Mr. Tom Hustler announced he understood the Grammar school were to leave Woodhill Lane and take up a new abode allowing the club to buy the field. Unfortunately this was not to happen in the foreseeable future of Mr. Hustler's tenure. The championship cup was presented by the Mayor to captain Syd Youren who in turn praised the performance of professional Rennie Nutter and presented him with a miniature cup containing a cricket ball. Mrs F Bland who had donated medals to the club presented these to the players.

Much of the praise for the championship winning side was given and rightly so to Rennie Nutter but Billy Williams should be commended. Bowlers are at their best when bowling in partnership and in Williams and Nutter this was an outstanding combination.

Billy Williams had come to live at Cross Cop, on the border between Heysham and Morecambe. Born at Darfield near Barnsley he began his cricketing career by playing for the village club at the age of 12. For five years he headed the clubs bowling averages before joining Mitchell Main in the Mexborough League. At this club he struck up a friendship with Roy Kilner who was later to play for Yorkshire and England. In 1911 Williams joined the Barnsley club as an amateur, taking 83 wickets at an average of 10 runs each. Developing as a superb slip catcher he then gained a place in the Yorkshire 2nd XI and subsequently made his debut for Yorkshire in that same year against Sussex at Headingley. In 1914 he played one first-class game for Yorkshire while playing as professional at Todmorden in the Lancashire League.

As the dark clouds of war gathered Williams joined the R.A.S.C. and spent three years in France witnessing the grim realities of war. Returning to England in 1919 he earned a place in the Yorkshire 1st XI and against Hampshire he clean-bowled eight Hampshire batsman and

North Lancashire League Champions, 1937
Standing L to R—W. Simpson, W. M. Forrest, P. Sission, R. Ratten, R. Nutter
Seated—F. Naylor, T. B. Hustler, S. Youren (Captain), F. Bland (President), A. C.
Williams, T. Hunt,
Front—H. Foster

took all but one of the ten wickets in their first innings for just 29 runs.
His friend Roy Kilner took the other wicket. In the Roses match he took
5-67 and figures showed he was comparable with the best in the
country at that time. *'The Visitor'* reported a unique feat involving
Williams when Yorkshire were due to play Leicestershire at
Huddersfield in July 1919. *'The Leicestershire team arrived at
Huddersfield a man short and Williams was asked to act as substitute.
Yorkshire winning the toss elected to bat. Skelding the bespectacled
cricketer claimed by many to be the fastest bowler of his time had him
(Williams) placed at second slip. It proved a most unfortunate move for
Yorkshire, for Denton, Rhodes, ,Burton and Wilson all presented their
erstwhile colleague with catches. Few men can claim a share of
dismissing four such players in one innings and the Leicestershire
captain gave Williams a bat to mark the auspicious occasion'.*

During this season he played when county commitments allowed as
professional for Slaithwaite in the Huddersfield League. 1920 and 1921
were spent at Haslingden after which he went to play for Royton in the
Central Lancashire League. He produced many remarkable
performances in League cricket but lacked one distinction – taking all

ten wickets in an innings. Playing for Royton a press report detailed when an opportunity had come *'He had claimed nine wickets and the last man had to face his bowling. The first ball hit the leg wicket and the bail fell, only to wedge itself in some unaccountable manner between the middle and leg stumps. The umpire gave the batsman 'not out' and another bowler took the last wicket.'*

His next engagement was with Aberdeen for whom he performed the hat-trick four times. He returned to England in 1925 to play three years for Darlington where he continued to display excellent form capturing over 100 wickets with 82 being clean bowled. From Darlington he then went to Heywood for 1928 and onto Ramsbottom for the 1930 season.
1931 saw him playing for South Kirkby and such was his respected views and knowledge of the game he wrote a series of articles for the *'Sheffield Mail'*.

His first experience of the North Lancashire League was with Barrow. His Morecambe colleagues would remember this as he scored a century against them and although Morecambe won Williams took four of the five wickets to fall in achieving their target. Although Williams was aged 50 in 1937 he was still contributing and played a significant part in achieving the clubs second North Lancashire League Championship. Employed at the ICI plant at Heysham he subsequently went on to play for the works team and upon retirement became groundsman at the Trimpell sports ground on Out Moss Lane for both the cricket and football teams.

This was a team that should be acknowledged as one of the best the club has ever produced. Although comparisons can be made with other years the influencing factors such as the standard of the league, the pitch, outfields, the performance of the professionals, overseas amateurs etc have all been discussed at some point in the bar. The legacy of Youren, Williams, Ratten, and Nutter take their place in the club's history.

To make it a memorable year the second team were runners up in Division One of the Westmorland League after promotion the previous year with Horace Hutchence and Tommy Cross Senior winning the batting and bowling averages respectively. The team repeated the feat in the following year with this time Geoff Garnett winning the batting and Walter Simpson the bowling averages.

The 1937 AGM discussed the issue of 'should women have a vote in cricket matters' Herbert Willacy and Frank Naylor supported the view.

Chairman Hustler agreed as they were full members and the meeting agreed to incorporate this provision into the clubs rules. A loss of £20 on the season left a balance of £9. Gate money was up and the cost of the professional had increased £30 more than the previous season. Gate money for the first team was £51 with the biggest gate £11 8s 3d against Kendal. Further talk ensued over the purchase of the ground once again.

The first team could not repeat the previous year's victory and finished in fourth place behind Vickerstown and Barrow who shared the title and Vickers Sports Club in third who were in their first season in the senior division. In the Higson Cup Morecambe lost their first round tie in extraordinary circumstances while playing at Parkside against Netherfield in an evening game. Finishing at 9.15pm in the farcical conditions of thunder and rain the Morecambe wicketkeeper was wearing a raincoat and all the other players were soaked to the skin.

Nutter was retained and he produced the form of the previous year to be the league's leading wicket taker with 92 wickets taking second place in the league averages.

Prospects for 1939 took a downturn when at the AGM confusion raged as Frank Naylor was elected as captain for the forthcoming season in place of Syd Youren. Thinking that as the present captain he did not need to be 'put forward' the members present voted for Naylor. No doubt this decision brought about Youren moving across the Lune to play for Lancaster in the Ribblesdale League. Members tried in vain to retain his services but there was to be no U-turn. Youren had an excellent first season scoring 399 runs at an average of 49.80 and a memorable game scoring 61 against Blackpool who had Harold Larwood as professional.

Frank Naylor was a most popular choice and the *'The Visitor'* reported: *'Apart from his outstanding ability as a player he combines shrewd judgment with a keen appreciation of the finer points of the game. Added to that, he is extremely popular with players and spectators alike, without in any way jeopardising the dignity and authority which his office entails. Finally he is born, bred and nurtured in Morecambe cricket and it is good to find a prophet honoured in his own country.'*

One new acquisition was W Lea, a left arm pace bowler and former professional with the Millom club. Lea was reported as being from Bournemouth and had spent a short period of time on the Warwickshire groundstaff.

A disappointing season ensued with a defeat to Netherfield in the first game. At Whit weekend there were defeats against Ulverston and Millom. On a Thursday night the Morecambe footballer Joe Read was included in the team but could not prevent defeat against Carnforth in the Higson Cup. Two wins against Millom and Carnforth with Nutter taking 8-20 and Lea 8-42 respectively relieved some of the gloom. Morecambe 3rd XI were bottom of Division Two of the Lancaster and District League with no win up to the end of July and in August on Bank Holiday weekend two defeats for the first team against C.M.S and Millom.

All this resulted in the side finishing second from the bottom of the league with just four wins. The remaining few games of the season were played out in a state of anticipation of the declaration of war. CMS cancelled their last match of the season as their players were needed to get buses ready for the transport of troops.

There was some good news as a crowd of 2,000 watched the Lancashire versus Yorkshire women's match in mid August, the last in a series of five games, Yorkshire scoring 82-9 and Lancashire winning with 83-6.

An Emergency Meeting of the North Lancashire League was held on the 10th February and clubs were asked to report on the prospects of fielding a team and issues around transport as the clouds of war gathered. Morecambe reported they would be able to put out a team but were pessimistic with regard to travel. Furness clubs discussed a 'South Cumberland League' but Morecambe decided to step aside and further meetings were held until a final decision taken at the meeting on the 17th May 1941 at the Barrow Working Men's Institute to suspend the league for the duration. The Secretary recorded that: 'the league be discontinued until more favourable circumstances arise'.

Cricket continued throughout the war at Woodhill Lane as the club put a team in the Lancaster and District League with a limited amount of clubs. In 1941 the club won the league and with it the Smith Trophy. Against Lansil Frank Naylor scored 117 not out as the standard of cricket was influenced by the availability of players attending to more important matters.

During the war the towns Midland Hotel became an R.A.F. hospital and throughout the war many of the convalescents were of a cricketing background. A number of county players played for the local RAF team. In the early part of the war the Reverend Tom Killick of Middlesex who had played two Test matches against the touring South Africans in 1929 was stationed in the resort and proceded to play in three games against Morecambe scoring 90 out of 163 of the RAF's score in the first game. Others players that played in various games were Arthur McIntyre of Surrey who later went on to play three Test matches for England and county players Hounsfield from Derbyshire, and Prentice from Leicestershire.

In July 1944 a match in aid of Hospital Funds was played between a Morecambe Past v Present. Captain of the Past was Fred Bland with the Present were led by Matt Forrest. A total of £50 was raised in a drawn game. Later that season the local hospital and the R.A.F. benevolent fund benefited to the amount of £18 each from a match between Morecambe and the R.A.F. The press reported this game took place in front of 800 spectators and the R.A.F. included the following County players Vigar from Essex, Blood (Notts), and Judge (Glamorgan), given that Morecambe had been given just 48 hours to put a team together the scores of the R.A.F. with 164-8 declared in two hours to Morecambe's 33 all out had a sense of inevitability before the game started.

The following year the R.A.F. played an Australian Air Force X1 at Woodhill Lane in front of a crowd of 600. Later that season Morecambe played Church from the Lancashire League. Another excellent crowd turned up to see Church score 203-5 declared. Church batsman Pilkington scored 76 and donated his £11 collection to local hospital funds. Morecambe replied with 181.

Chapter Five — Ribblesdale League Cricket

1946 was a slow start to post war cricket. Morecambe rejoined the North Lancashire League together with Lindal and Kendal. In addition Morecambe seconds would compete in the Lancaster and District League.

Secretary of the club was Tom Hartley who announced he would be relinquishing the post at the end of the season. Since 1913 he had been a tireless worker for the club and was well respected by many of the players who had passed through the club. Tom Hartley played for just one year for the club's 2nd XI in 1912 when they were members of the Lancaster and District League. In 1946 they were back in the local league after a brief period in the Palace Shield. A teacher at Euston Road School for 27 years he retired in 1938. Hartley had been a member of the committee since 1913 an unbroken run of 33 years and this had been his second period as secretary. He had previously acted in that capacity for a period of three to four years during the 1920's, resuming the role in 1941 when Mr. F Siddle was called to the forces. Throughout the war years Hartley had been instrumental in keeping the club together and now with the first year of post war cricket in the North Lancashire League a further challenge was upon members of the club.

Frank Naylor who had joined the club in 1924 was to return to the club. In 1927 he made his first century against Heysham on a Bank Holiday Monday scoring 110 runs in a partnership of 130 with Reg Dean. His most recent was against Lansil as previously mentioned in 1941. Later that year he joined the Army and served two years in Burma suffering serious illness. This was now to show itself in the post war seasons as he not only battled the bowlers but the effects of the illness as well. A prominent footballer Frank had previously been a member of the Old Thornton Athletic Football Club.

Dick Ferguson was engaged as the club professional. Ferguson was from Yorkshire and his achievements were not confined to the cricket field. He had a collection of trophies for running, darts, football and bowls. Over the Pennines he had played cricket in both the Yorkshire Council and Bradford Leagues during the war, and before that he was well known in the Midlands. Taking over as groundsman at the club together with his playing role the field's condition had improved.

Ferguson started his career with Whitwood Colliery, where he was employed as a miner, under the supervision of Cecil Tyson of whom he described as the best left hander Yorkshire ever had. Tyson is one of the select band of players to score a century on his first class debut. From there Ferguson went to Thurncroft in the Bassetlaw League staying for five years. He then moved to Wynbush in the Birmingham League being professional until 1935. Next he played for Gainsborough being the groundsman as well at The Rose Brothers County Ground. In 1941 Ferguson was then directed back to the mines and his cricket was played at the South Kirkby club in the Yorkshire Council League staying until the end of last season. On five occasions during that previous season he had played for Windhill in the Bradford League in a star studded team led by Les Ames, Kent and England wicketkeeper, also included was George Dawkes the Leicestershire and later Derbyshire wicketkeeper, Bill Voce, and Ellis Achong the West Indies Test player. In the last of his two seasons he had taken 70 and then 85 wickets before then agreeing to be Morecambe's professional.

The opening game of the season was against Furness and although Ferguson had the memorable figures of 7-10 he still ended up on the losing side as Morecambe could only muster 32 to a Furness total of 79 all out.

The first victory of the season was against Vickers SC and their formidable professional Haydn Nutton. Ferguson captured the prize wicket and with Vickers dismissed for 82 Morecambe won by two wickets, Ferguson scoring 26 to complement his 6-24. An excellent Whitsuntide weekend saw victories against Ulverston on Saturday and Whitehaven on the Monday.

In early June *The Visitor* reported the club having difficulty in obtaining accommodation for Ferguson. As a result Ferguson resigned his position and on June 15th was due to play his last game when a stranger talking to Tom Cross in the pavilion that Saturday offered a solution allowing Ferguson to complete the season.

Up to June 29th Ferguson had taken 58 wickets and finally completed a highly successful season finishing with 76 wickets at an average of 8.7 runs each. In addition he scored 293 runs, which was the highest in the team in a season which many clubs were finding their feet after the Second World War.

In the team of 1946 was Jimmy Britton a local footballer who had played mainly for Morecambe Reserves in the 1937/38 and 1938/39 seasons although he did make 16 first team appearances. Then having played for Lancaster he turned professional after the war playing for

Bradford Park Avenue and Rochdale. Britton had played cricket locally before the war and joined the club in 1946. After one game in the second team he was promoted to the first team and took a season's best 8-28 at Haverigg.

At the North Lancashire League AGM of 1946 on the afternoon of Saturday October 26th the meeting was informed by the Morecambe representative Mr. J Checkley that he had just been informed by telephone that the club had been accepted into the Ribblesdale League and as a result would be leaving the league.

Member clubs of the North Lancashire League had always considered the Morecambe club to be isolated geographically and membership had always had a hint of irregular attendance indeed the clubs membership record of 1902-04,1906-09,1921,1927-39 and 1946 gave a good indication of 'easy come, easy go'. The club had always been at the most southern tip of the league and journeys to Whitehaven, Cumberland Motor Services, Haverigg and Millom were time consuming even by train.

The club's AGM of 1938 recorded an unsuccessful application to join the Ribblesdale League and with the news that the club was now about to venture into a new league eight years later the clubs secretary Alan Hartley suggested it would involve less traveling and a higher standard of cricket. The addition of Morecambe put the Ribblesdale League membership up to sixteen clubs. The format was that the clubs would play 22 matches each. Clubs were split into two sections, Morecambe's consisting of Lancaster, Blackpool, St Annes, Leyland, Leyland Motors, Chorley and Darwen. Clubs in the same section played home and away. The other section consisted of Settle, Blackburn Northern, Great Harwood, Barnoldswick, Clitheroe, Ribblesdale Wanderers, Whalley and Read. These teams would be played just once.

Uplifting the standard of the clubs cricket Morecambe 'A' resigned from the Lancaster and District League and rejoined the Westmorland League. The club's second team were to stay in the Westmorland League until the formation of the Northern League. The 'A' team showed they could compete with the best the league could offer and in 1948 two club individuals headed the league averages. Matt Forrest headed the league's batting averages with 492 runs at 35.14 and Arthur Wilkinson took 69 wickets at 5.52 a piece. In addition the club announced it would run a midweek team playing on Wednesday evenings to develop some of the younger members.

The 1946 AGM had certainly included significant changes within the

Ted Whitfield,
Morecambe Cricket Club
Professional 1948 and 1949

Eddie Paynter
Lancashire and England, who
played for the club at the start of the
1949 season

club's league membership and the club felt it was appropriate to recognise the following members, Mr. H Hartley, Mr. R Parker, Mr. L Noble, and Mr. RW Bibby with life membership as new optimism was evident. One member even suggested the club should make enquiries to sign Maurice Leyland.

Come April next year however Dick Ferguson had been retained as the club's professional and the side struggled to make any impression in the new league as they finished bottom of the league for the first two seasons. For the 1948 season the club's prospects seemed to be on the up as the engagement of Ted Whitfield the ex Northamptonshire and Surrey all-rounder raised members morale. Whitfield had been top of the North Lancashire League batting averages the previous season while playing for the Whitehaven club. Optimism grew further when 'The Visitor' reported Ellis Ratcliffe a former Lancashire League batsman was joining the club together with Alan Marshall a pace bowler from Bingley.

Whitfield's performances were such that by the end of May the club had offered him terms for the following season. Bottom of the league, the highlight of the season was Ellis Ratcliffe scoring 103 not out against Leyland Motors at Woodhill Lane. Whitfield finished the season with the excellent figures of 571 runs at an average of 31.72 and 69 wickets at 11.66 while Gilbert (Geoff) Stones had the credible bowling figures of 44 wickets at 13.34 as the club took its second consecutive wooden spoon.

Whitfield agreed to terms for the following season and prior to the start of the season the former England & Lancashire batsman Eddie Paynter was reported in 'The Morecambe Guardian' as being available to play for the club.

Paynter had been professional at Keighley since 1940 and had been released through mutual agreement as he was looking to manage a public house in the area. First game of the 1949 season was away at Clitheroe. Paynter must have wondered what sort of a side he had come to play for as Morecambe batting first were dismissed for 37, George Hudson the Clitheroe professional taking 7-22. This was a season Hudson would take a record 124 wickets. However a dramatic turn of events with Paynter keeping wicket, a new bowler to the Morecambe ranks, G Spencer took 6-15 as Clitheroe succumbed to 35 all out and victory to Morecambe by two runs.

The following week came victory against Settle with Paynter scoring 71 not out earned the former England man a £4 collection. Professional Whitfield not to be outdone scored 43 and took 3-35 with the ball. Victory against Great Harwood by one wicket with Whitfield taking 5-21 set up the derby game against Lancaster.

A disastrous performance with the bat followed as Morecambe folded to 61 all out and Lancaster earned victory by eight wickets. Frank Warne the Lancaster professional taking 8-23. The Lancaster club took a £79 gate as the local public watched Warne at his best and Paynter in grim fighting mood.

This was the last game Paynter played and the following weekend being Whitsuntide saw Morecambe lose to Chorley on Saturday and tie with St Annes on the Monday. During the St Annes game at Woodhill Lane a most unusual incident occurred when a pigeon flew into the scorebox. Found to bear a ring with a Marton (Blackpool) address the pigeon was secured and taken back by the St Annes team on their coach with a view to reuniting it with its owner.

The club's form then deteriorated as the season progressed. A crowd of 3,000 saw Morecambe lose to Blackpool at Stanley Park and in the return fixture at Morecambe Whitfield was injured. He was replaced by the Australian professional at Rawtenstall, Frank Freer. The home side progressed to 88-1 with Freer 58 n.o. netting himself a £10 17s collection before rain curtailed the game. A gate of nearly £39 was reported as one of the best ever for the club as attendances increased.

The last game of the season resulted in victory against Darwen with Jim Haigh taking a memorable hat-trick in that all his victims were LBW. It was almost by accident how the club discovered Haigh. During the war on holiday in Morecambe he came to watch the cricket on a Bank Holiday Monday. One man short Haigh stepped out of the crowd and offered to play explaining he had experience of playing in the Yorkshire Council League and so began a long association with the club. Jim Haigh lived in Bentham and worked at the Silk Mill travelling each week to play and despite his efforts in that last game of the season once again the club finished a disappointing 12th place finish.

Further bad news was that Whitfield was to leave the club to take up a player coach position at Ebbw Vale in the South Wales League. *The Visitor* reported that although he would be away in the summer Whitfield in partnership with his brother-in-law Mr. FG Mitchell intended to take over a fancy goods and tobacconist in the town with a view to developing a sports equipment outlet.

Ted Whitfield's career developed through playing schools cricket in London, then through the South African GA Faulkener's cricket school. He was offered a contract to join Surrey in 1929. Professionals on the staff at that time were Jack Hobbs, Andy Sandham, and Herbert Strudwick, the finest English wicketkeeper at that time. The amateurs playing were Percy George Fender and Douglas Jardine later to captain England on the famous and controversial Bodyline tour. This was the thirties and class distinction was still prominent with the amateurs dressing rooms upstairs at The Oval and the professionals downstairs. Even when playing away on tours the two groups stayed at different hotels. Whitfield's chances were restricted and indeed after scoring 198 against Cambridge University on his debut he was dropped for Jack Hobbs return from Test Match duty. The retirement of senior players allowed him to establish himself as an integral part of the side and in 1939 he scored over a thousand runs after which he was presented with his county cap. The Second World War robbed him of his prime years as a batsman and in 1946 he joined Northamptonshire for one year. From then onwards he dropped into the leagues and developed his talents as a coach. This was a role in which he was to gain great respect and many admirers. During his time at Morecambe Whitfield's presence resulted in up to sixty youngsters turning up for practice at Woodhill Lane - a number never seen before and in later years he returned again to coach while professional at Netherfield.

The club wasted no time in engaging a new professional for the 1950 season. Yorkshire slow left arm bowler Alan Mason was appointed before the end of September. Mason had played with Addingham from the age of 14 before moving to Keighley after Army service. In 1948 he had played for Saltaire and in the year prior to his engagement at Morecambe he had been professional at Pudsey St Laurence in the Bradford League.

The AGM of 1949 showed a financial balance sheet with £93 in the bank. Debate at the meeting centered on the ground rent increase from £17 to £54 and the fact Sunday cricket was still not allowed on Woodhill Lane. Members agreed that club representatives should approach the Trimpell club with a view to hosting exhibition games as the prospects of good cricket and financial benefit should be explored.

Fleetwood were newcomers to the Ribblesdale League in 1950 and Padiham rejoined having been absent since leaving prior to the outbreak of World War One.

The opening match of the season saw defeat against St Annes 57 v 59-7 with Mason taking 5-25. The next two weeks were washed out and then victory against St Annes in the return fixture 134 v 75. Jim Haigh scored 100 not out in the victory against Leyland Motors (171 v 176-3) but the season's results were up and down with heavy defeats against Blackpool (30 all out) and Blackburn Northern (34 all out). Victory against Ribblesdale Wanderers 126-9 declared v 72 all out saw captain Geoff Stones have the excellent bowling figures of 7-16 from 5.6 overs. And two wins from the last two games both against Fleetwood, who finished bottom in their first season, gave Morecambe an equal 10th place finish.

In October a major announcement from the club that Australian Harry Lambert was to be the clubs professional for the 1951 season. Lambert was to become the club's first overseas professional. The club chairman Mr. R Parker was quoted as saying that *"supporters were demanding a better class of cricket and the club was trying to see if we would get the promised support"*. This was a huge gamble in that Lambert was to be paid twice as much as any other previous Morecambe professional. The reported figure was between £25 & £30 per week. Gate money had been down to £168 from the previous year's record of £281. The club was hoping Lambert would pull the crowds back in. A total of £1500 was going to need to be raised in the winter to supplement the new signing together with the cost of other cricket expenses during the season. Social secretary Jack Satterthwaite was to arrange a Christmas Raffle, followed by a Whist Drive culminating in a mammoth finale, plus an amateur talent show at Whitsuntide on the Central Pier.

Lambert had been professional at Ramsbottom the previous two years. An Australian from Victoria, Lambert had played Australian rules football for the Collingwood team, but it was cricket he excelled at most of all. After making his Sheffield Shield debut in the 1947/48 season he went on to play for the Commonwealth X1 on their tour of India and Pakistan in 1949/50.

At the start of the 1951 season 'The Morecambe Guardian' reported not on finance or the playing side of the club but the fact that the other most essential ingredient of a successful season the tea ladies were in short supply. With no bar or alcohol license, catering was a valued income and the Lancashire County Education Committee rejected an application from the club to play a West Indies XI on a Sunday afternoon to further dampen the clubs spirits in raising funds.

GEOFFREY STONES, MORECAMBE C.C

Les Baxendale

Morecambe's captain all-rounder

A scheme for installing seats, presumably in anticipation of increased attendances, the club decided to set aside a small area in a memorial park dedicated to the memory of former cricket enthusiasts. Relatives of such people would have the seats installed.

Geoff Stones was to be the club captain with Frank Naylor his deputy. Alan Hartley was elected second team skipper.

While Harry Lambert set off on the high seas aboard the S.S. Strathaird on the 6th March the club revealed another major signing in that the former Lancashire and England leg spinner Len Wilkinson was to play for the club.

Another addition was Jack Dunbar a policeman from East Lancashire who had transferred to Morecambe with his employment. Dunbar had previous experience with Church in the Lancashire League.

Wilkinson's career was something of a fleeting acquaintance with cricket at the highest level. In 1938 Wilkinson had a growing reputation as a leg spinner and up to the start of August he had taken 87 wickets in 26 matches. Lancashire then defeated Kent at Canterbury with Wilkinson taking match figures of 12-125 followed by a glorious late summer finale finishing with 151 wickets and winning himself a place on the England tour to South Africa that winter. Although he was fourth choice spinner he played in three of the tests and topped the tour averages with 44 wickets at an average of 18.86. Wilkinson was at the top of his game.

Starting as a seam bowler with Heaton in the Bolton League at 15 he then turned to spin. Trials followed at Old Trafford where he was offered an engagement enabling him to give up his job in a cotton mill. In 1939 he took 63 wickets for Lancashire but under performed in comparison to the previous year. South Africa was his peak.

After the war he returned to Old Trafford to restart his career. Injured in the first match of 1946 he had a cartilage operation and could not play until 1947. A hot dry summer in which he only appeared in two games he then duly retired from the county scene at the age of 30. Back into the leagues he was professional for Furness in 1948/49, Settle in the 1950 season, and was to now team up with Harry Lambert as an amateur in a formidable bowling partnership as the 1951 Ribblesdale League season beckoned.

Lambert arrived on the 16th April and after a few days in London was pictured in 'The Visitor' arriving at Euston Road station greeted by the club president Dick Blacklock and the chairman Percy Sissons.

The first game of the season was against Leyland Motors and defeat by eight wickets but by the first week in June after nine games talk of winning the championship was in the local papers as Morecambe were placed fifth with Read leading the table. The following week Frank Warne the Lancaster professional took 8-97 in a drawn game, Morecambe scoring 205-9 dec and Lancaster 96-7. Heavy defeats then followed against Chorley and Blackpool as the title challenge faded. Lambert's performances were steady if not always match winners and by late July club officials had opened talks with him about re-signing for the following season.

Len Wilkinson, Lancashire and England
Joined Morecambe in 1949—pictured in the nets at The Oval

Defeat in the return fixture against Blackpool. Then Lancaster scored a convincing victory at Woodhill Lane. Partial recovery beating Padiham by 70 runs in a game Jim Haigh scored an undefeated 62 and Lambert taking 6-44. Despite 59 from Lambert the side encountered defeat at home against Darwen. In the Darwen side that day playing as an amateur was a sixteen year old on the Lancashire Ground staff by the name of Brian Booth later to play 350 First Class games for Lancashire and Leicestershire. Having taken 53 wickets up to the middle of July he was then selected for the Lancashire second eleven whereupon the Ribblesdale League notified Darwen they could no longer play Booth as he had in their view become a 'professional'.

At Settle an encouraging win was brought about by Lambert who scored 80 not out and took 6-45. A rained off game against St Annes, followed by a drawn game against Read at home, before rain intervened again to bring the game against Ribblesdale Wanderers to a premature end. The fixture list brought about the final two games to be against Fleetwood. In the 1950 season Morecambe won both these games, twelve months on exactly the reverse happened.

Morecambe finished in much the same position as the previous season with a playing record of seven wins, five draws, and ten loses. Chief weakness was the batting. The arrival of Dunbar and Wilkinson strengthened it but not enough. Haigh and Marshall supported Lambert in the bowling and Wilkinson after a shaky start had been an asset to the side.

In the middle of the 1951 season skipper Geoff Stones left the club after receiving a promotion in his employment. Stones was an engineer and had been Lancaster's professional in 1946 when he was signed from Hanging Heaton in the Yorkshire Council League. The experienced Frank Naylor took his place as captain.

Throughout the season gates were down on the levels required to break even. The biggest draw should have been the Lancaster game. Two seasons ago when Whitfield was the professional on £10 a week this match gave Morecambe a £100 gate. When all the expenses had been paid the club was able to bank £98. This season's gate was £46, with refreshments and raffle contributing £20.

This was the first time the club had paid a lot of money for a professional. An expense, which had been a big drain on the clubs resource's resulted in the AGM for the 1951 season showing the following finances.

Gate receipts totaled £289, an increase of £121 on the previous season. Subscriptions increased by £57 to £302 plus the donations for the seats. Catering brought in £99 as against £58 and social functions £388 compared with £184. On the expenditure side professionals wages were £454 and the groundsman's wage £145 compared with £173 and £148 respectively. A loss of £132 was recorded on the season.

What of Lamberts performance? With the ball he took 71 wickets and after a poor start with the bat with some wild hitting he tempered his rashness, and by a judicious mixture of caution and aggression scored 443 runs. If he had batted at number three or four in the order instead of opening he would probably have scored more runs.

The club and player could not agree terms for the following season and after protracted negotiations Lambert returned to Australia.

A bright and promising start to the season gave way to a fitful season ending on a dull note and the notable signing of the clubs first overseas professional had not repaid the faith the clubs committee had put in both the members of the club and the residents of the town.

The most important event of the year was to come to the surface in November of that year as the Ribblesdale League faced a major crisis. The membership was now at 18 clubs and clubs could only play five teams twice. This had caused discontent among many clubs. At the Ribblesdale League AGM held at Whalley representatives from North Lancashire League clubs Furness and Kendal were in attendance as a proposal that a Western section be formed consisting of Blackpool, Chorley, Darwen, Fleetwood, Leyland, St Annes, Lancaster, Morecambe, and Leyland Motors who had not been involved in the preliminary discussions, plus Kendal and Furness. In proposing the motion Mr. JC Higginson of Lancaster said: *"We have heard quite a lot about secret meetings but I want you to forget that. We have had this change in mind for a number of seasons and it was necessary for us to get together and go into the possibilities of a Western Section. The best way to do this was for us to have an informal talk among ourselves and duly advised the President of the situation"*

Emphasis was put on no split was intended and in the minds of the proposing clubs the league in its present formation meant the fixtures were unbalanced. The vote was nine each and the League President used his casting vote to defeat the proposal. The President emphasized he was not happy with the situation, two clubs had been persuaded to resign from their league and the other nine he said had 'put a pistol to the heads of the officials. In response Mr. Higginson said Kendal and Furness had not been approached initially and their club's representatives said they had been *"kicked out of their league"*. The votes had been cast, however, and the eight clubs resigned from the league and left the meeting. Leyland Motors had concern over the way the issue had been handled but felt obliged to go the same way as they were in the same geographical encampment. The split was complete and later that Saturday in a Whalley Hotel the 11 clubs met and formed The Northern Cricket League.

Chapter Six — Northern League Early Years

The club needed to focus on the financial issues which were left after the previous season. After the inauguration of the breakaway section of the Ribblesdale League to form the new Northern League it was only a couple of weeks after the formation that the club gave notice of the new professional for the 1952 season.

George Walsh a 35 year old all rounder was the new incumbent, a less than high profile signing. Walsh had played for Clitheroe in the previous season scoring 764 runs and taking 74 wickets. In the 1937 and 1938 seasons he had played for Rishton in the Lancashire League moving on to take up the professional position at Cupar, Scotland before the outbreak of the war. Post war he had then played for Arbroath in 1947/48 and Brechin in 1949/50 before returning to Lancashire.

Morecambe were led by Jack Dunbar in their first game in the Northern League. This resulted in defeat against Leyland by eight wickets. Leyland had Les Warburton the England trialist as their professional. A feature of the season was the high percentage of drawn games and the following week a rain affected drawn game against Blackpool reported public schoolboy David Keighley showing promise against the ex-Sussex player Jim Parks who was the paid man at Blackpool.

A defeat against the eventual first winners of the league St Annes was clouded in controversy when Ellis from the Fylde team claimed he had caught Len Wilkinson inside the boundary. Wilkinson was going for his third six and the vociferous home supporters let it be known they thought Ellis was over the line. The umpire conferred with the fielder and Wilkinson was given out, to which Morecambe folded to 107 all out and victory for St Annes by 4 wickets. Les Warburton scored 87 not out in the return game against Leyland who scored 143-6. In reply Jim Haigh and Keighley put on a century opening partnership before rain brought proceedings to an end. Against Kendal Len Wilkinson took 5-54 and scored 50 not out in another drawn game. On June 11th the first victory of the campaign was earned against Leyland Motors with 171 against 127 and Len Wilkinson again to the forefront with 63 and 6-52.

The first Northern League match against Lancaster was played over two nights, Morecambe getting the better of another draw scoring 109 and Lancaster replying with 99-9. Jim Haigh scored 52 and Dick Ferguson having the excellent figures of 7-2-11-6. Both received collections of £4 5s and £6 5s respectively. In the drawn game against Fleetwood Wilkinson took 6-67 and proceeded to score 22 off 4 balls when called upon to bat hitting three sixes and one four before being caught off the fifth ball he received. Professional Walsh had a benefit game in which West Indian Test Player Clyde Walcott hit Len Wilkinson for 38 in one eight ball over, five sixes and two fours.

The club hosted a Lancashire Federation game against their counterparts from Essex in August. Victory resulted for the Red Rose county scoring 192 v 128. Included in the Lancashire team was future England batsman Geoff Pullar. A Morecambe Grammar School pupil Brian Fletcher was included in the Lancashire team. Also playing for the Lancashire Federation in 1952, 1953, and 1954 was a future Morecambe professional, Colin Gradwell. As the season came to a conclusion Jim Haigh who had performed well with the bat scored 101 out of the side's 155 all out against Darwen. It could not prevent defeat however and Morecambe lost by six wickets to finish in seventh place out of the eleven original clubs who formed the league.

In November at the AGM anxiety about the financial position were discussed as moves to ban lotteries and raffles was in the news. Percy Sissons the club chairman announced the signing of Jack Parker the ex-Surrey player and when asked *"on what terms'"* he replied it would not be proper to release the details but he had signed for *"a very reasonable figure'"*. A loss of £95 on the season brought the total deficit to £227. A number of atrocious Saturdays with the weather had meant they never had a gate above £30 he added. Jim Haigh and Len Wilkinson took the 1st team batting and bowling awards with Harry Ashton and Alan Hirst for the second team. Jim Haigh was then elected captain for the following 1953 season.

With the signing of Jack Parker as the club's professional for 1953 an air of expectancy was around the club in late April. Parker a Surrey stalwart who had just retired from the first class game after 340 games, had been working as a salesman in the winter was expected to arrive in Morecambe on the Tuesday prior to the first game at home against Furness.

Arriving as expected he told *'The Visitor'* that the ground looked good and the players promising. It was his intention to bring his wife and two little girls aged nine and five but thought the weather would be too bad. Admitting he had misjudged the weather as the sun had shone for most of the month he added: *"if the weather stays the same I can see myself enjoying Morecambe very much"*. Parker came from Battersea in

Morecambe CC 1953
Back Row, L-R, D. Youren, G. Fairbrother, ———, ———, J. Normanton, ———,
———, K. Williamson.
Front Row, L. Wilkinson, J. Parker (Pro), P. Wardlaw, K. Brooksbank

the shadow of the Battersea Power Station chimneys where he played his early cricket. Leaving school he worked in a shipping office with the Shaw Saville Shipping Line. The call of the sea was hard to resist and in 1928 he sailed all over the world working on the liners. The depression which hit shipping in 1930 made him move more towards a cricket career. Surrey had been after him for a number of years and in 1930 he signed as a professional.

Jack Parker's Surrey career spanned 20 years from 1932 to 1952. A top order batsman he was a more than useful medium pace bowler whose performances were restricted later in his career by a troublesome back which during the next two years was to give him further problems at Morecambe. Parker never played Test cricket but had good trials in 1932 and 1933. In 1934 he lost his place in the Surrey side not regaining it until 1937. In 1938 he scored his first century and the following year was his best as he scored 1,549 runs and took 56 wickets at 22.38 runs apiece.

In 1939 he was picked for the MCC tour of India but this tour was cancelled due to the outbreak of war. He joined the RAF as a Physical Training Instructor finishing his service with a Royal Australian Air Force Squadron. After the war in 1946 he was top of the bowling averages and the following year he headed the batting. A permanent fixture up to his retirement he had the satisfaction of winning the County Championship with Surrey for the first time since 1914 in 1952. *'The Visitor'* asked Parker what did he consider his major highlights of his career He replied he took pride in his 255 against the New Zealanders in 1949 which was the highest score against them by an Englishman. Against Kent at Blackheath he took eight catches, a record for Surrey and of course the Championship title. Parker was complimentary about Lancashire saying he *"enjoyed playing against them. Always did well against them and thought they were grand and generous players".*

"Cricket is easily the best game for character building. Like life, up one day down the next," he added. The best players he had played against were *"Bradman a batsman in a class of his own, slow bowler Bill O'Reilly and Larwood the best fast bowler".*

Parker celebrated his 40th birthday at Morecambe on the 23rd April followed by the opening game against Furness which resulted in a draw, Morecambe making 109-5 in reply to a Furness score of 179-9. Parker took 3-49 and scored 33 with the bat, 24 runs coming in one over.

Against Leyland Motors at the end of May a high scoring game saw victory for Morecambe by six wickets. West Indian Lloyd Messado scored 99 in 89 minutes before being bowled by Len Wilkinson had allowed the Motormen to declare at 210-8. In Morecambe's reply of 211-4 Jack Parker scored a magnificent 134 not out but it was a newcomer who took the plaudits as well. This was Keith Williamson's first game. Coming to join Parker with the score at 176 his contribution was only nine not out but by rotating the strike Parker was able to see them home.   As the two left the field the spectators headed for the pavilion to clap Parker from the field.

Williamson had previously played with the Great Horton club in the Bradford League and had transferred to Morecambe in his employment with the Halifax Building Society.

The following week was Coronation Day and the local derby game against Lancaster at Lune Road. Officials, members, and players lined up before the game to sing the National Anthem which was followed by

Jack Parker
Surrey CCC and Morecambe Professional, 1953 and 1954

a resounding three cheers for the Queen led by Captain John Sanderson of the Lancaster club. Parker and Ken Brooksbank opened the innings for Morecambe and re-wrote the record books with an opening partnership of 146. Parker went to score 107 not out before a declaration with the score at 246-3. Parker's efforts earned him a £5 collection from the spartan crowd who had endured the wintry weather. The game ended in a draw as Lancaster finished on 127-5. Parker was displaying all his experience and continued his rich vein of form by scoring 52 in the return game against Lancaster although Morecambe suffered defeat.

Against Darwen at the end of June Parker showed true sportsmanship as when he was caught on the boundary edge by a spectacular catch he applauded the fielder as he departed. Parker's benefit involved other professionals playing in the league such as Indians Ramchand, Palwankar, Dhwandi and West Indian Ken Rickards. J Oakes, the ex Sussex player who was playing at Rochdale also played and £33 was raised from the game. Against Blackpool, Morecambe got their first taste of the great Bill Alley who scored an undefeated 126 in Blackpool's score of 177-1 before the rain brought an end to proceedings.

Jack Parker had scored 688 runs a record which was to stand for more than 30 years. He was well supported by Ken Brooksbank, Jim Haigh and Len Wilkinson. Wilkinson who also took 53 wickets at an average of 15.08 runs each created an amateur record which would stand for the next 37 years.

A sixth place finish in the league which had now seen the addition of the Preston club from the Liverpool Competition to bring the membership up to 12 clubs.

The financial position of the club had been somewhat eased by the hard work of the social committee who had raised over £500 and as a result the club had a bank balance of £30 with no overdraft. Wages of the groundsman and professional had decreased by £100 but gate money was much the same as the previous season. Suggestions at the AGM that players should pay for their own tea and that a new scoreboard built were passed. One member commented that the scoreboard was the worst in the league and that some clubs in the Lancaster and District League have better ones. It was also decided to withdraw from the Tower Shield due to the shortage of wickets on the square.

A good crowd turned out for the first game of 1954 against Fleetwood at Woodhill Lane. Jack Dunbar had moved to Lancaster and included in the Morecambe side was HB Mossley, a wicket-keeper from the Airedale and Wharfdale League. An all round performance from Keith Willamson with 46 not out and 4-15 plus Len Wilkinson taking 5-63, gave the home side victory by two wickets. After his run scoring feats the previous year Jack Parker opened with a 'duck', but it was an eye catching performance of quick bowling by Fleetwood's new professional West Indian Roy Miller who took 5-68 and whose bowling was described by The *'Morecambe Guardian'* as *'devastating'* that made Morecambe officials take note. Further victories against Furness and Leyland pushed the side up the table until defeat against St Annes and an announcement that Len Wilkinson was to leave the club. Wilkinson had bought a newsagents business in Barrow and hoped to get the necessary permission to play for Barrow in The North Lancashire League. The season tailed away with Parker unable to emulate his success of the previous season and the club finished again in sixth place.

Early in the season a drawn game against Leyland saw the remarkable feat of the Leyland professional and ex England trialist Warburton out in the first over against Morecambe c.Mossley b.Farebrother 0. Nothing unusual in the dismissal but this was Warburton's first 'duck' in five years.

At the end of the season the club had accumulated a £96 debt but good news was that a Christmas competition which would raise £80 and with the Corporation rebate of £25 the club would be solvent again. Bad weather prevented Parker's benefit game taking place but the club still had to pay him a guaranteed benefit of £121. This was in addition of an increase to his wages by £53 to take his wages for the season to £218. Gate receipts had dropped £68 to £184 but good income from socials was keeping the finances in the black.

At December's AGM Percy Sissons the club chairman announced the signing of the six foot three inch Jamaican fast bowler Roy Miller. Miller who as previously mentioned had played for Fleetwood in 1954 had been offered terms but declined. Fleetwood's replacement was amateur Will Greenhalgh who was playing for Radcliffe in the Central Lancashire League. A contributing factor of Miller's decision must have been that the Fleetwood club had finished bottom of the league with just three wins. Miller played seven first class games for Jamaica and one Test match for the West Indies against India in March 1953. *The Fleetwood Chronicle* in January 1954 unfolded the story that Miller had signed for the Fleetwood club on the recommendation of Everton Weekes, who was playing in the Lancashire League for Bacup. The paper reported Miller was to play against the touring MCC and added that if picked for both games he would probably play in the First Test due to begin on January 15th.

Miller did play in both games leading up to the Test but was not selected for the Test team. In the first game he bowled first change taking just one wicket in an innings defeat and did not bowl in the second game on a slow low wicket that made runs and wickets hard to come by resulting in a predictable drawn game. Two poor performances probably cost him his place and these were to be his last two first-class games in the West Indies as he left the Caribbean for the Irish Sea and the fishing port of Fleetwood. Miller had a 55 wicket haul in his first season on English turf and had then agreed to move up the coast to Morecambe for the 1955 season.

Phil Wardlaw was captain and in his first season Miller took 66 wickets but it was the additional bonus of him scoring 493 runs that made him a tremendous signing for the club. Eric Townson, a policeman, joined the club from Lancaster and Gordon Farebrother went the opposite way. Jim Haigh was still playing and 15 year old David Garner began to score runs in the second team. To keep up with appearances the club was presented with a new flag by Mrs T Altham of the neighbouring

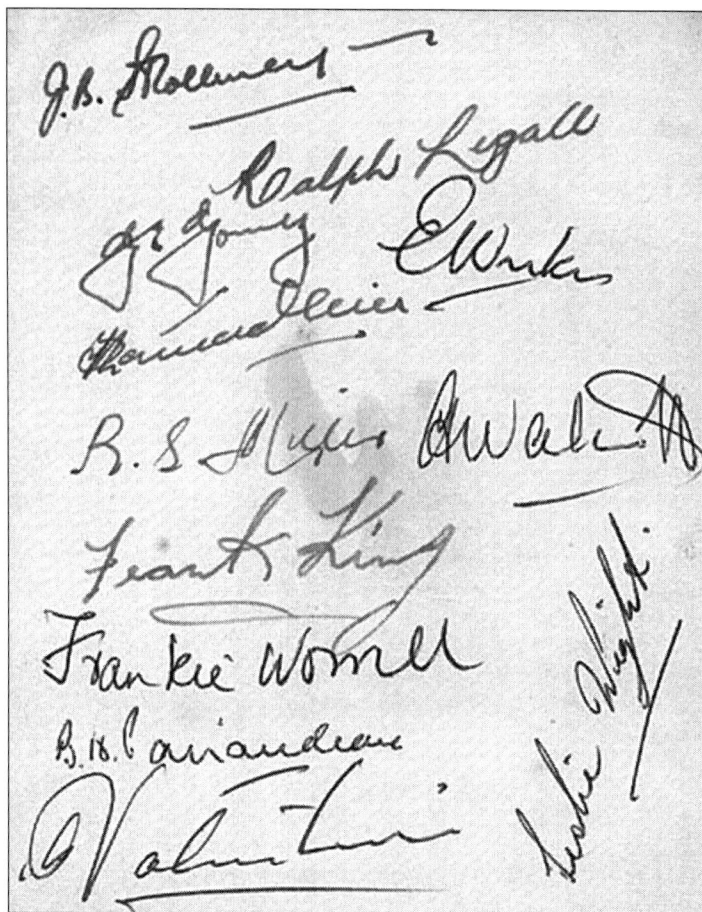

A collection of autographs from the only Test Match Roy Miller played including Worrell, Walcott and Weekes

Woodhill Farm. The flag was designed in the club's colours of Maroon, Green, and Gold with the monogram of MCC. In early May Morecambe's game at St Annes was the only one to go ahead on a cold and wet day which had seen the game at Kendal snowed off. After early morning rain, a thin covering of snow formed on the pitch shortly before the start. In contrast on a glorious hot sunny day later in the season Miller blasted Darwen away with a 7-39 haul, and in the 2nd XI fixture at Woodhill Lane. HB Mossley slayed the Darwen attack for 130 in a Morecambe total of 203-5, this after Darwen had declared on 199-5.

H.B.Mossley	b.Garner	130
A.Neave	b.Monk	6
G.Parkin	c.Kay b.Monk	33
R.Meadows	b.Monk	0
J.Smith	b.White	1
F.Normanton	Not Out	11
A.Marshall	Not Out	18
	Extras	4
	Total for 5 wkts	203

Against Leyland also in the second division R.Cropper took a hat-trick and four wickets in five balls finishing with 5-37 in Morecambe's defeat with Morecambe 98 all out, Leyland 101-5.

In early June Chairman Sissons was quoted in the *'Lancashire Evening Post'* as saying that it cost *"£70 a week to run the club. Not until Whit Monday had the club taken a gate over £20 and this was more than the last three home games takings put together. In a season we have to take £300 gate money and even then we have to find a lot more"* Highlight of the 1955 season was a victory over champions Blackpool. This was their only loss of the season. In late June the *'Lancashire Evening Post'* wrote: *"Through style and speed of his deliveries frequently damages heels of his boots. Last week Miller had to come off when the heel came away from his boot. No boots in the changing room would fit. Not even those of the clubs lofty chairman Percy Sissons. The defective boot was rushed to a local cobbler but by the time it was returned Morecambe were at the crease."*

A match was arranged in liaison with the Local Tourism Board and the Manchester Sports Guild for the visit of a Pakistan Eaglets team to play a Northern League X1. The aim of the Guild was to raise money for a new sports stadium while fostering links with amateur cricket clubs. The Guild's intention was to give some of the profits from the game to the Morecambe club. Poor weather prevented any sort of a gate and it was only because of tickets sold in advance that the event broke even. Gate receipts for the season went up to £198 with biggest being £40 against Blackpool with who Bill Alley was professional and the lowest of £4 against Darwen. Club Chaiman Percy Sissons announced at the AGM that if there was not an improvement in the financial position of the club the future looked uncertain.

Phil Wardlaw was again in charge for 1956 with Arthur Marshall second team captain. The first game of the season was defeat against the previous season's champions Blackpool for whom Bill Alley wasted no time in getting back into the groove with 110 not out.   Geoff Stones

PAKISTAN EAGLETS

CRICKET TOUR 1955

MORECAMBE SECTION
Presented by
THE MANCHESTER SPORTS GUILD

FRIDAY, 2nd SEPTEMBER, 1955
AT
MORECAMBE C.C. GROUND
Woodhill Lane, Morecambe

WICKETS PITCHED 11.30 a.m.

PAKISTAN EAGLETS
v.
A NORTHERN CRICKET LEAGUE XI

OFFICIAL PROGRAMME - 6d.

Organised by THE MANCHESTER SPORTS GUILD, Head Office:
460 WILBRAHAM ROAD, MANCHESTER 21, with full co-operation
from THE MORECAMBE CRICKET CLUB and W. M. MARSHALL,
ESQ., PUBLICITY OFFICER, TOWN HALL, MORECAMBE.

Front cover of the programme for the match between the Northern
League XI and the Pakistan Eaglets, 1955

was back in the Lancaster team who beat Morecambe in the first round of the Slater Cup by the slim margin of one wicket. Against Furness Miller took the first nine wickets and only Ken Brooksbank taking the last wicket prevented him capturing all ten. In the last game of the season against Blackpool Bill Alley again scored a century this time 140 not out taking his total for the season against Morecambe to an undefeated 250. Despite this the club finished in equal fourth place with Blackpool. Miller took 61 wickets this season to finish second in the leading wicket-takers with Roger Garlick the former Lancashire and Northamptonshire player, now professional at St Annes, out in front with 63. An all round team effort with the bat resulted in contributions from David Keighley 172 runs, John Neave 353, Miller 343, Keith Williamson 353, Ken Brooksbank 324 and David Garner 236.

Percy Sissons the club Chairman addressed members at the AGM in February to reflect on the 1956 season and reported a bank overdraft of £268. Gate receipts had dropped from £198 to £125 and socials had only raised £293 in comparison with £471 the previous year. There was criticism of the league in the way the fixtures had been arranged with four successive away fixtures in June and bad weather for the five fixtures in July. The following seasons were a lot better, he added. Roy Miller's benefit had only raised £43 and although Test players had been playing there was a poor attendance.

Mr. A Farrer remarked he could not understand a decrease in subscriptions of £11 and suggested an appeal be made through the local press. New people were coming to the town and many new houses were being built, he remarked. The Secretary and Club captain reported that the first team had finished in its best position in the league since its formation although the second team had been disappointing there were a number of promising young players who had progressed well under the guidance of Monday night coaching from Ted Whitfield. Whitfield was professional at Netherfield in 1956 and 1957 while they were still in the North Lancashire and District League. Wardlaw concluded by adding that Miller had been engaged again for the 1957 season. Matt Forrest asked "*if clubs would be able to fulfill fixtures if petrol rationing continued*". This question was raised in relation to the Suez Crisis and the club secretary replied that there should be no difficulty in traveling but mowing the field may be a problem. It was agreed the Secretary would write to the Regional Petroleum Officer for an allowance.

The Northern League and Lancashire County Cricket Club entered into an agreement for the start of the 1957 season. This was on the basis

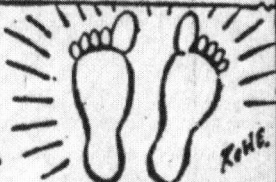

that the County would supply the clubs with a player from its groundstaff to act as the club's professional and receive payment from the club. This was an arrangement that did not endear itself to the majority of clubs but Lancaster, Chorley, Preston, Leyland and Fleetwood signed up for its inauguration. To emphasise the extremities of the arrangement Lancaster won the league and Preston finished bottom. Some of the County staff played for at least two clubs in the season and when two of the clubs in the agreement were playing each other it was not unheard of two players arriving not knowing which club they had been assigned to. At which point the toss of a coin generally settled the matter.

At the end of the season four Lancashire County players headed the bowling averages but it was Roy Miller who had the leading wicket haul with 83 victims. Morecambe finished joint fourth from the bottom with an identical playing record to that of Kendal. No other Morecambe bowler had a five wicket performance or qualified for the league averages telling something of the performance of Miller with little support from the other end. Willamson, John Neave, Brooksbank, and Miller all scored over 300 runs with Ken Brooksbank's 73 not out the highest score of the season. Morecambe seconds finished bottom of the table a position that was to be duplicated the following season, Mike Willis hitting four fifties and Hedley Giles with 390 runs their main contributors.

Secretary Phil Wardlaw told the AGM at the Victoria Hotel in early 1958 there was a real potential the club may have to leave the Northern League due to the cost in providing cricket. Although there had been a working profit on the year and the overdraft had been reduced to £144 this was due to the Social Committee who had worked tirelessly. He then added *"the club needed to obtain permission for Sunday Cricket, move to another ground or go out of existence as a Northern League club. A move to a lower grade of cricket with no expense required for a professional should be considered. We are the only club without a bar and efforts are needed to obtain a bar"*

Chairman Percy Sissons said it was getting to the serious stage and members would have to work hard if they were to have a club in the future. From last years debt of £322 had been decreased to £263 and since the balance sheet was audited it was now down to £144. Treasurer E Moore gave an example of the apathy in the town in that the gate receipts on Cup Final day were only £2 1s 8d. On four occasions less than £10 was taken on the gate and this when the club had paid £50 for new cricket balls. Percy Sissons explained that the President Fred

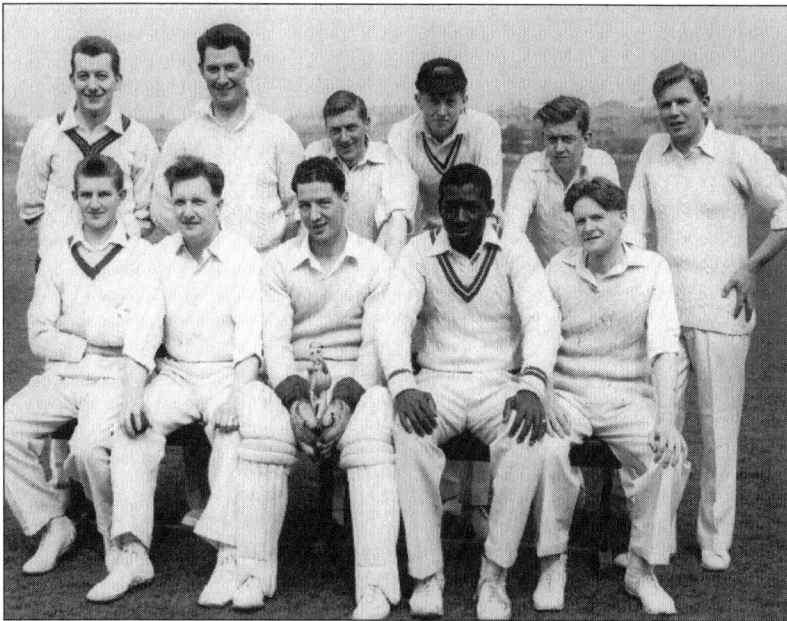

Morecambe Cricket Club 1st XI, 1956
Back Row L-R, J. Normanton, B. Cauwood, J. Neave, ———, A. Neave, ———.
Front Row, D. Garner, K. Brooksbank, P. Wardlaw, R. Miller (Pro), K. Williamson.

Bland had paid for the new scorebox. If this had not been forthcoming then there would not have been one. Roy Miller had agreed to return for 1958 with a guaranteed benefit of £75 and at the conclusion of the meeting Mr. J Satterthwaite who had been a committee member for 34 years was made a Life Member. Satterthwaite had played football for Morecambe, joining from Barrow. He played in the 1921/2 and 1922/3 seasons before leaving to play for other local teams.

Prior to the 1958 season the club received the welcome news that its application to play Sunday games had been granted. The Education Authority permitted two Sunday games for the new season. 1958 was a dismal season as the club hit rock bottom with both teams finishing at the foot of their respective divisions, although it could be said that the first team had five wins the same as sixth placed Lancaster they picked up very few of the bonus points on offer that season. Miller toiled away again to take 72 wickets and finish second in the leading wicket takers behind his fellow West Indian fast bowling Jamaican Tom Dewdney who took 84 wickets for runners-up Darwen. This was to be Miller's last

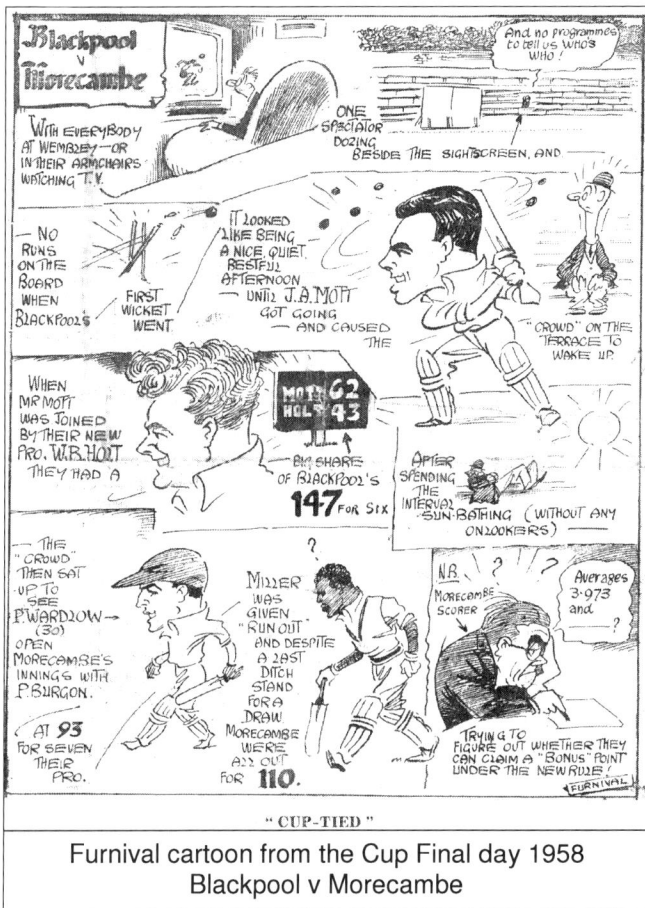

Furnival cartoon from the Cup Final day 1958
Blackpool v Morecambe

season at Morecambe after four very successful seasons and the club and player parted on amicable terms. After failing to agree terms Chorley stepped in to sign Miller. Miller repaid Chorley by taking 82 wickets in becoming the league's leading wicket taker the following season when they finished runners up.

At the AGM in January 1959 the club reeled from the blow of seven resignations which included Chairman, Sissons, Treasurer Moore, Kitchen the Social Secretary and four other Committee Members. Benny Birchall, a Director at Morecambe Football Club was elected Chairman and 16 year old Joseph Cowper elected Treasurer. Moore who had been in the position for eight years reported that the overdraft was

Matt Forrest, Morecambe CC

down slightly to £133 and informed the meeting that Morecambe were the only club in the Northern League who had made a profit, although gates had been down again. Mr. Jack Orkney said the club needed to get out of the red and into the black, and instead of paying rent secure the ground by purchase. In response the President Fred Bland said they had talked about purchasing the ground for the last 30 years but it was not easy. Mr. Orkney said the football club had held Sunday matches after the cricket club had declined. £100 had been raised and the cricket club should reconsider.

One of those other committee members was Matt Forrest who resigned after 30 years in which he had served as Committee Member and Treasurer. He had started playing for the club in 1929. Matt Forrest was a schoolmaster at Sandylands and remembered the day Walter Bell burst into the classroom where Forrest was teaching and with the permission of Councillor AW Gorton the headmaster he was to leave the class and travel with the Morecambe team for a Higson Cup match. Forrest found his kit had already been packed and the coach was outside waiting. He left and scored 50 for the team.

In his school days Forrest attended Lancaster Royal Grammar School but rarely made the school first team. After attending St Johns Teacher

Training College in London he picked up his first teaching appointment in London and played for Edgware. On his periodic visits to Morecambe he played for the club and on his permanent return to the borough he became a regular and was captain in 1932. He was the backbone of the club through the Wartime and played after the war for the club in the Westmorland League.

As Matt Forrest stepped down from the committee the new election of officials included the name of Paul Speak who was to serve the club for the next 50 years in almost every capacity of officialdom.

In 1959 Netherfield joined the Northern League with Furness moving back to The North Lancashire League. Netherfield had a difficult first season and finished bottom of the league.

The *'Lancaster Guardian'* reported in April before the start of the season that Albert Shuttleworth the club's scorer for over 40 years was to retire. Shuttleworth who lived on Primrose Street was regarded as a master of his craft and the paper reported *'he would be missed by colleagues and friends around the grounds.'*

Keith Williamson was to lead the team in 1959 with Mike Willis second team captain and Doug Melville was to be the club's professional. Melville had been at Vickers Sports Club in The North Lancashire League previously. Ray Jagger, Dave Duncan and Michael Robinson from the Lancaster & District League joined the club. Ray Jagger had previously played for Halton in the Lancaster & District League taking 91 wickets in 1955 the year of their promotion to the first division and 81 wickets in 1957 their only first division championship before the club folded prior to the start of the 1959 season. J Simpson another newcomer from Lancashire League club East Lancashire was included for the first game which was washed out.

The following weekend Morecambe entertained Blackpool and the prolific Hanif Mohammad who was the Seasiders' professional and then held the record score for a Pakistan batsman of 339 against the West Indies in the 1957/58 series. For the Blackpool game Morecambe included Singhalese all rounder L Williams and Ray Jagger. Hanif Mohammad was caught behind by Phil Wardlaw for just 16 as Morecambe gained a rare victory over the Stanley Park outfit by scoring 157-9 declared. Ken Brooksbank scoring 64 and Peter Burgon 50. Blackpool replying with just 64 all out, Doug Melville taking 3-26 and Dave Duncan 4-34. Duncan's time at Morecambe was short lived, however, and he went on to have many successful years at Lancaster.

In June Freddie Moore from the Lancashire groundstaff deputized for the injured Melville and took 6-54 against Darwen in a drawn game. Morecambe had to wait until the 13th June for their second victory of the season against Netherfield and in July against Kendal both sides observed a minutes silence for former committee member Mr. WU Tyson who had died earlier in the week.

Ken Brooksbank scored 587 runs, a club record which was to stand until 1983, and Ray Jagger was the club's leading wicket taker with 37 wickets. Club professional Doug Melville performed admirably with bat and ball as the first team finished fourth from bottom. In a move to reduce traveling costs the club bought a 26-seater coach from local travel operator Harrisons for £160. A saving of £80 a season was expected on travel expenses.

In October the club held its first Dinner Dance for ten years at The Grosvenor Hotel with 100 guests in attendance.

The club successfully applied for an increase in the council grant scheme and £25 was increased to £50. This was approved in November but only by the narrowest of margins in a 14 to 13 vote.

Chapter Seven— The Sixties

At the AGM in January 1960 the club announced a balance of £163 with the overdraft paid off. The purchase of the motor coach had not however been successful as the purchase and running costs amounted to £147. The sum of £40 was however recovered when the coach was sold.

John Normanton was back playing after a two-year lay-off and Phil Wardlaw moved across the River Lune to Lancaster. In the first second team game of season against Leyland Hedley Giles scored a memorable 143 out of a total of 199-8.

Keith Williamson was skipper of the first team and with Ray Jagger taking 8-45 and 6-14 in consecutive weeks against Darwen and St Annes respectively made for a promising start. In addition for the first time in ten years the club progressed to the second round of the Slater Cup by beating Netherfield. In late May a ten wicket defeat was inflicted on Morecambe by Blackpool for whom the opening partnership of Edmundson and Hanif Mohammad had not been separated for three weeks. A defeat by Chorley included the club's former professional Roy Miller who scored 89 and took 5-38 in what was to be his last season in the Northern League.

Victory against Kendal in the Slater Cup set up a semi final against Darwen, who after defeating Morecambe went on to defeat Blackpool in the final. The season tailed away with defeat in the return match with Blackpool for who Hanif Mohammad scored 115 not out. In the next to the last game of the season away at Darwen the game was completely rained off and with no prospect of any play the team went to Ewood Park to watch Blackburn Rovers play Spurs.

The first team finished joint seventh with the second team having their best finish since the formation of the league in fourth position. J Simpson took 63 wickets, a record which was to stand for the next 30 years and with Fred Normanton scoring four more runs than Hedley Giles the previous season he became the highest runs scorer for the second eleven.

The 1961 season had for the first time a league game on a Sunday, this was against Lancaster at Lune Road. Playing Sunday matches at Woodhill Lane was still ruled out by the Education Authority. Extensive work in treating the square with marl had been undertaken in the winter months and the club hoped this would provide hard fast wickets producing brighter cricket. In addition the club also made improvements to the seating arrangements by the purchase of some large forms.

Doug Melville was to be professional again and a poor season saw the first team finish next to the bottom of the league with the second team finishing rock bottom. Highlight of the season was David Garner scoring 123 against Kendal but even this failed to secure victory, Morecambe scoring 195-8 declared and Kendal replied with 200-2. Blackpool 'pro' West Indian Rohan Kanhai topped the batting averages scoring 919 runs and former Lancashire and Somerset bowler Jerry Hilton in his second season at Fleetwood topped the bowling with 77 wickets.

In December 1961 at the club's Annual Dinner at The Grosvenor Hotel the Deputy Mayor Councillor TF Higginson announced he hoped the Lancashire Education Committee would soon relax its ban on Sunday cricket. In addition he announced a festival of sport was proposed to be held in the resort over the last two weeks of June and the Corporation was expecting the support of the Cricket Club in hoping to arrange matches. The Deputy Mayor paid tribute to the work of the President Mr. Fred Bland and club officials announced that Doug Melville would be playing as an amateur for next season.

At the AGM in January Club Chairman Roy Killip made a plea for more players. Indoor nets were to be held at Preston again as the players had felt they had been of benefit. A lot of money had been spent on a new mower and the reconditioning of the old one. Treasurer Paul Speak quoted £806 income for the 1961 season up from £440 the previous year. This had paved the way for a £323 profit. Gate receipts dropped to £70 £40 less than last year and the football sweep had brought in £400. The club was to be involved in a great deal of expense as consideration needed to be given to the replacement of seating and sightscreens. In complete contrast to the Annual Dinner members were told there had been no contact with regard to Sunday Cricket nor any mention of a Festival of Cricket.

1962 will be remembered for the tragic events off the field with the car crash which killed the captain Ken Brooksbank. Returning home from a game at Netherfield on July 7th the car collided with a lorry and then a bus about four miles outside Kendal on the A6 near the Heaves Hotel. In the car was Ray Jagger who suffered a fractured skull and chest injuries, Gordon Wearing had severe head injuries, John Barratt cut by flying glass and Lancaster's Kevin Higgins who had been playing with

Annual General Meeting at the Victoria Hotel, 1960

their second team at Kendal had face cuts. Ken Brooksbank died in Preston Infirmary after being transferred from Kendal Hospital for a brain operation. Brooksbank was in his third season as captain. He had been captain in 1957 and 1958 previously. A Yorkshireman he joined Morecambe in 1952 after previous experience with Bowling Old Lane and Saltaire in the Bradford League moving to the town to work at Morecambe Press.

Prior to the season Morecambe engaged a new professional WH (Bill) Dean, a right arm fast medium bowler. Dean had previously played just one game for Somerset against the touring Indians in 1952 with no success and in 1961 he had been playing at Stockport. Maurice Jagger was to be second team captain.

At the start of the season Dean was ill and Morecambe brought in Ken Howard from Lancashire to 'sub-pro' for the first three weeks. After the first set of fixtures was washed out Fleetwood inflicted a heavy defeat on Morecambe and Dean's return and debut against Lancaster was eagerly anticipated. Batting first Morecambe could only score 105 and in reply Lancaster won by five wickets. Bill Dean's form was poor and because of this an agreement was made with the club he would resign his position as professional and apply to continue to play as an amateur. The league refused this permission. All this took place shortly before the tragic events of July 7th 1961 at which point Dean then re-

Pic 25   Morecambe CC 1st X1 1962 Back row Left to Right K. Howard (Pro), D. Garner, C. Thompson, J. Cowper, R. Jagger, H. Giles, Front Row. F. Normanton, H. Clarkson, K.Brooksbank, D. Burgon, G. Wearing.

approached the league who then gave the go ahead. Traveling from Yorkshire each week he paid for his own expenses.

The games on July 14th saw all clubs at first and second team level in the league observe a minute's silence for the memory of Ken Brooksbank. Morecambe's game against Chorley showed a much-changed team with new professional for the rest of the season Gerry Houlton included in the line up. Although Morecambe gained a victory, their first of the season by 11 runs, 158 v 147, Bill Dean taking 5-62 and a good all round performance from Houlton scoring 53 and taking 4-23 cricket seemed to be the last thing on people's minds at that time.

The club set up an appeal fund and donated £50 to its initial start. Other early contributions were received from the Vale of Lune RUFC, Bill Dean, and Gerry Houlton donated his collection from the Chorley game.

Gerry Houlton finished the season with 658 runs just 30 short of Jack Parker's record in 1953 with an average of 50.62 from just 14 innings. The second team struggled and finished next to the bottom of the league from out of which John Normanton created a new record batting aggregate of 563 runs, which would stand for the next 30 years.

A loss of £139 on the season was reported to members at the AGM. Members stood in a minute's silence for Ken Brooksbank before Gordon Wearing gave his report as Secretary. Inviting players to come and play for the club he guaranteed them of a warm welcome and then thanked Alan Butler the former secretary who had stood in for him after the motor accident. Paul Speak gave the treasurer's report and told members the appeal fund for the road accident had totaled £915 thanking everyone who had contributed he said: *"it was heart warming to see the way individuals and other clubs had rallied round us".* Chris Thompson who had been captain of the team since the death of Ken Brooksbank had been with the club for four seasons since his move from Lancaster was elected to continue as first team captain. John Normanton was to captain the second team.

Ken Bennett was engaged as the club's professional for 1963. Bennett had been an amateur with Furness in 1953 before moving into the paid ranks in 1955 and played with Leyland Motors up until 1962. An all-rounder he was taking around 40 wickets plus around 400 runs a season. He fitted the club's budget. Doug Melville was still playing as an amateur, Ray Jagger and Gordon Wearing were back into the fold, and with Guy Lunn, a forcing batsman joining the club from Lancaster the club could look to try and escape the clutches of basement league positions.

This was not to be and the first team finished bottom of the league with just one win. Bennett scored over 500 runs and took 33 wickets but more essentially there were no five wicket-plus hauls that win games. Doug Melville was the highest wicket taker with 38. Another notable performance that season was Frank Wilkinson scoring his first 50 in the first team that season.

Bennett was re-signed for the following season and prior to the new season the press reported Charlie Clough was to join the club from the Bare club in the Westmorland League. For the previous three seasons he had won the club batting averages and in 1962 scored two centuries which was some achievement given the dominance of the ball over bat in local league cricket at that time. A change of captain to Ray Jagger did little to change the playing fortunes of the side although they did

Gerry Houlton
Lancashire CCC and Morecambe CC,
1962 and 1965

win four games as opposed to one the previous season.

In June the club suffered a blow when it was announced Doug Melville would not play again that season as he had had several teeth extractions and not been well since the treatment. This was to be Melville's finale after some valuable service and he left with a bizarre incident that season when playing Darwen he sub fielded for the opposition and ran out Guy Lunn. Towards the end of July the club announced it would not be resigning Ken Bennett who then proceeded to score 56 against Leyland Motors, 83 against Chorley, and 60 not out against St Annes on Bank Holiday Monday. With only two games of the season remaining the club announced Gerry Houlton who had stepped in with much success in 1962 would be the professional for the 1965 season. Both Clough and Lunn scored just over 300 runs but leading run scorer for the season was Frank Wilkinson with 388.

Ex Lancashire player Houlton had played the majority of his first-class cricket in 1961 when he made 16 County Championship appearances but since then he had played mainly Second X1 cricket with just one Championship and one Gillette Cup game in 1963. Leaving Lancashire at the end of that season he then took up an appointment as professional with Middleton in the Central Lancashire League for 1964.

1965 was to be a memorable year as the club was to win its first Northern League trophy since the inception of the league in 1952.

A newcomer in 1965 was the Reverend Jeff Yates who had taken up a position in the resort at the Sefton Road United Reformed Church. Charlie Clough took over the reins as first team skipper and in the first game against Chorley ex Lancashire captain Joe Blackledge 83 and Frank Henry with 80 not out allowed Chorley to declare at 212-3. In reply Morecambe stumbled to 115-6 with Houlton making 52.

The first team won just two games in finishing second from the bottom of the league. Gerry Houlton scored 584 runs and was the highest wicket taker for the club with just 26. This was to be the side's main problem in that they could not bowl out the opposition as from the 22 games played 12 were drawn. The second team performed a little better in that they finished fifth from the bottom with ironically four bowlers in the top thirteen of the second division averages.

Where as the league was a disappointment, a victory in the first round of the Slater Cup against Netherfield gave the club a bye through to a semi-final tie against Chorley. Overturning the early season league defeat by batting first Morecambe scored 185 with Ken Beal 47, Frank Wilkinson 44, and Gerry Houlton 32. Chorley fell short by 21 runs making 164.
This set up the final against Leyland Motors. 'The Visitor' reported there should be a record crowd for the final and after poor weather in the week prior to the final the sun came out to greet the teams. A crowd of 500 did indeed attend and winning the toss Morecambe elected to bat. Frank Wilkinson and Gerry Houlton put on 119 for the first wicket and with Hedley Giles making 31 in 12 minutes including two successive sixes a total of 199 was set for the visitors. Excellent bowling by all the Morecambe bowlers with excellent catches by Hanson and Giles restricted the Motors to 119 all out.

The large crowd gathered around the pavilion to see Mr. William Blackledge the League Chairman present the trophy to Charlie Clough.

After the euphoria of the cup win one of only two league wins in the season was on Saturday August 11th against Lancaster, Morecambe scoring 253-4 through Wilkinson 44, Clough 82 not out, Lunn 29, and Beal 34.

Lancaster's reply was just 70 with Houlton taking 7-28. After the game Houlton informed the club he would not be taking up the clubs offer to continue as professional for the following season. Houlton told *'The Visitor'* that *'He did not know if he would continue to play as a 'pro' in league cricket.'* Houlton paid tribute to his teammates by adding *'They are the best set of lads I have ever played with and I have played the game all over the country.'* The following week Houlton scored 106 in the drawn game against Leyland. Speculation circulated as to who would be the next 'pro' and the club announced Norman Fell, a 29 year old medium fast bowler who lived in Harrogate and had been a professional at Undercliffe in the Bradford League for a number of years would play the last two games of the season with a view to taking up next season's position. Fell scored 28 and 25 with the bat but failed to take any wickets in the final game of the season. In the last second team fixture of the 1965 season against Kendal ex-first team skipper Phil Wardlaw turned out and scored a creditable 25 as the seconds finished on a high note winning their last four games.

Tragically in 1965 President Fred Bland died in a Blackpool hospital. Mr. Bland had been a former player with the club in his earlier years following in the footsteps of his father, captain of the 1927 side, and his grandfather who played on the formation of the club in 1889.

Fell must not have produced enough to earn himself a contract as at the club's annual dinner it was announced the ex Lancashire bowler Ted Kelly would be the club's professional for 1966. Kelly's Lancashire career had been limited to just four first-class games in 1957 while he had played several second XI Minor Counties games in 1956. Kelly had been professional at Chorley from 1961-64. Mr. Laurie Boyden who had stepped in as President since the death of Mr. Fred Bland presented each player from the trophy winning side with a cap. Mrs. V Bland donated a Rose Bowl to be presented to the clubs best all-rounder and Ken Beal was the first winner. Prior to the start of the 1966 season Charlie Clough replaced the score box, which had been smashed by vandals in the winter. This was to be the start of a trend that would bring the club's ageing pavilion to its knees as constant vandalism took its toll.

New President Laurie Boyden was already President of Undercliffe Cricket Club in the Bradford League. A businessman with interests in various engineering companies in Bradford he appealed to the Vice Presidents and Patrons of the club for donations to put the club on a sound financial footing. A poor season again saw the first team finishing second from the bottom. Kelly's best performance was 8-38 in a nine wicket over Leyland Motors. Jim Cumbes was 'pro' for Chorley taking 4-11 in one of Morecambe's defeats out of a total of 30 all out. Again it was the cup that raised hopes of success as wins against St Annes and Leyland Motors brought a home semi final against Preston. With the largest crowd of the season a tight game ensued and Morecambe lost by the small margin of eight runs, 122 v 114. *The Visitor* gave a mid season report on professional Kelly that he *'was pretty innocuous, lacking penetration, and accuracy. Although Kelly is a trier of the highest order he is past his best as a fast bowler.'*

In July Guy Lunn left the club to play for Carnforth in the North Lancashire League. Lunn who had joined the club from Lancaster in 1963 was to join up with Dick Bradley the ex Lancaster 'pro'. Lunn scored 1,148 runs with his most notable performance being 87 off the Chorley bowling in 1964.

Again there were only two victories in the league season, one of these being against Lancaster with Kelly taking 5-38. The second team made it a double the same day with Ian Hanson taking 6-18 as Morecambe scored 152 and Lancaster replying with 90. Lancaster did however have revenge in the first team return fixture winning by four wickets. Ted Kelly informed the club he intended to emigrate to Australia and the club would need a different professional for 1967.

The Reverend Jeff Yates was captain for another season of difficult times as the club lurched from one crisis to another. Tom Gifford, a seasoned cricketer from Ulverston in the North Lancashire League took up the mantle of professional for the club. Poor weather early season resulted in the first game against Fleetwood being washed out. The first home game against Kendal resulted in defeat by four wickets, Morecambe 36 all out although Ray Jagger took 5-13 in Kendal's 37-6. On May 24th '*The Morecambe Guardian'* headline reported '*Club may be forced to quit League'*. This headline was maybe a little rash but the background to it was the poor weather. The article quoted a cost of £28 a week to field two sides in the Northern League. Gate receipts of just £8 had been taken up to May 24th because of the rain. To run successfully the club needed £1,000 per year. Starting the season with £300 in the bank the club had lost £130 in the first five weeks.

On the playing side it took until the first week in June before the side scored over one hundred, this being 115 in the one wicket defeat against St Annes. A let-off against Netherfield with the Cumbrians 89-0 and Bob Entwistle the former Lancashire opener stranded on 58 not out in reply to Morecambe's 113 all out when the rains came. A surprising win against the previous years champions Darwen with scores of 114 v 98 was followed by defeat against Preston when Morecambe had to play with no professional due to an injury to Gifford. Gifford's form had been poor and the club turned to the Lancashire County Ground staff to fill the vacant position while Gifford was injured.

Lancashire sent David Hughes, later to have a long and distinguished career for the county, for the game against Netherfield. Hughes took 7-16 but this was not enough to prevent defeat as Morecambe could only score 62 in reply to Netherfield's 104. One of the county's favorites Duncan Worsley deputized for the derby game defeat against Lancaster and in the last game of the season a victory over Chorley saw David 'Bumble' Lloyd take 4-39 and score 40 with the bat. Hughes ended the season at the top of the league's bowling averages as his short stay had seen him take 17 wickets at 7.64 runs apiece. Since Gifford's injury the impact of a professional contributing to the side's performance had raised morale and needless to say Gifford was not retained for the following season as the club was on the eve of a miraculous upturn in its playing fortunes.

Chapter Eight — 1968 And All That !

The club was in poor shape financially in the late' sixties and although the Slater Cup victory in 1965 had been an injection of success the club's annual task in the league had mainly been to avoid the wooden spoon. The pavilion was in a poor state of repair and with football being played in the winter on the far side of the ground this provided a challenge for any fielder with the rough ground. With the Education Authorities still using the ground for school sports events line marking on the outfield was clearly evident for a large portion of the season.

From this background a turnaround in the clubs playing fortunes was something of a minor miracle as the First XI won the League and Cup double.

Back at the helm as club captain was Charlie Clough and engaged as the club's professional for 1968 was Colin Hilton, the former Essex and Lancashire fast bowler. Hilton's career had started in his hometown with Atherton Collieries Cricket Club where he had received coaching from WH Davies the former Glamorgan player who had played against Morecambe as the Netherfield professional in the early 'thirties. Playing for the Lancashire Federation in 1954 and 1955 Team Manager Jim Gledhill said of Hilton: *"I think without doubt he was the fastest bowler who ever played for us and what a workhorse"*.

Hilton was recruited as a seventeen year old to the professional's job at Ribblesdale Wanderers where he took 8-88 in his first game. It was in 1955 that he first played for the County 2nd XI progressing to his first-class debut in 1957. Hilton continued his progression into the 1st XI attack and quickly earned a reputation as one of the fastest bowlers on the county circuit. With Brian Statham a regular in the Test team he was able to gain further exposure. In 1961 Lancashire went from being runners-up the previous year to finishing in 13th place although this was a successful season for Hilton as he took 75 wickets. In 1962 Bob Barber was relieved of the captaincy duties and replaced by JF Blackledge who was playing his cricket in the Northern League for Chorley and well known by the Morecambe players, officials and supporters.

Blackledge had only been playing for the county seconds occasionally and it was assumed by the cricket committee his management of the players would reverse the county's fortunes. The county only won two games out of 32. Hilton played in 30 of these games and was awarded his county cap while capturing 87 championship wickets and making his career best score of 36.

At the end of that terrible season Joe Blackledge retired from cricket, Bob Barber moved to Warwickshire and Ken Grieves who had left prior to the start of the season to play in the Central Lancashire League was brought back with the opportunity to lead the county.

With England due to tour Australia in 1962/63 much of the national press were speculating as to the possibility of Hilton being included in the touring party. This was not to be as he needed knee surgery and a longer than expected recovery period meant he only played in five games for the county in 1963. With Brian Statham coming to the end of his Test career and the emerging Peter Lever Hilton's time at the Red Rose County had come to an end.

Hilton's career with Lancashire ended with a total of 91 appearances and 263 wickets. Trevor Bailey was the captain of Essex and arranged for Hilton to join the county for the 1964 season. A far from successful season followed with Essex finishing in mid-table and Hilton taking just 25 Championship wickets.

Colin Hilton then returned back to the leagues and joined Oldham in the Central Lancashire League for the next three years. Released from Oldham his next stop was Woodhill Lane on the 'Lancashire Riviera'.

Colin Hilton
Lancashire CCC

The opening game of season against Darwen was cut short by rain but not before a certain player listed as A.N.Other on the original team sheet had signaled his arrival by scoring a century. That player was Roger Wrightson a 28 year old wicketkeeper batsman who had played County cricket for Essex up until the previous season. President Laurie Boyden had brought him to the club and Wrightson's debut score of 113 contained 12 fours and six sixes. Batting first Morecambe scored 202-5 declared to which Darwen progressed to 62-5 before rain intervened. Colin Hilton took 4-21 in conditions far from favorable for fast bowlers.

Onto Fleetwood and a remarkable game with Morecambe batting first and making just 49. Ken Snellgrove from Lancashire was 'sub pro' for Fleetwood as the contracted professional Robinson was not available. Hilton bowled superbly taking 8-9 and aided by two top class catches by Wrightson as Fleetwood were dismissed for 38.

Defeat in the third match against Leyland Motors brought the team back down to earth but the following week victory against Netherfield in the Slater Cup first round when Hilton, bowling from a shortened run up due to a muscle strain got the prize wicket of ex-Lancashire opening batsman Bob Entwistle playing on. The Derby match at Lancaster was won by the narrow margin of two wickets with four balls left, and after a rain affected drawn game at Netherfield victory came against Preston with Kenny Beal taking 6-18. By beating Chorley on Whit Monday this put Morecambe to the top of the table with Netherfield. The next few games saw wins against St Annes and Netherfield but defeat in the return against St Annes in a low- scoring game of 79 v 66.

With receiving a bye through to the Semi Final of the Slater Cup this brought opponents Preston who themselves had received a bye after dismissing Lancaster for 34 in the first round. The first scheduled date was washed out and the following week after Hilton had taken 8-13 in the defeat of Leyland on the Saturday. David Hughes, sub pro for Leyland took 5-36 and scored 17 in Leyland's 55 all out. A star performance by Alan Jagger taking 4-18 was instrumental in defeating Preston by 69 runs for whom a young Adrian Robinson scored 25; he was later to become a Morecambe professional.

A defeat to nearest challengers Blackpool in early July with Hilton not at his best and Wrightson missing through a bad back was a setback but this was cushioned with the news that Hilton would be back as 'pro' the following year and the following week Kendal were crushed by 156 v 32, Hilton taking 7-12 and making 51 not out with the bat.

On the Sunday the Slater Cup Final was held against Leyland with 700 spectators in attendance at Woodhill Lane. Leyland could only make 74 as Clough 4-26 and Hilton 3-9 were well supported in restricting the visitors. Winning by four wickets Morecambe stumbled over the line with Bill Bland hitting a six to win the game. As the first team were receiving all the plaudits it became slightly insignificant that on the 27th July the second team recorded their first victory of the season in defeating Chorley.

1968 Championship and Slater Cup Winners
Back Row, L-R, Mr O. Pithers, R. Mashiter, D. Hastings, W. Bland, K. Beal, J. Binns, R. Sandam, R. Jagger, G. Robinson, R. Killip.
Front Row, Mr P. Speak (Chairman), F. Wilkinson, C. Clough, C. Hilton (Pro), H. Giles, B. Pratt, (Scorer)

A defeat to Leyland brought main rivals Blackpool to Woodhill Lane. Morecambe batted first and made 143. In reply Blackpool were on the verge of defeat at 47-8 when West Indian Test player Charlie Stayers decided to hit his side out of trouble. Stayers made 43 but could not stave off defeat and Blackpool finished at 104 all out. Hilton's 6-50 earned him a £10 collection. It was in this game that Wrightson was credited with two stumpings off Hilton. Northrop & Maley decided to combat Hilton's pace by taking guard out of their ground, but to their embarrassment as soon as the ball passed them Wrightson the wicketkeeper was removing a glove and hurling the ball at the wickets to stump the two Blackpool batsmen.

A drawn derby game with Lancaster meant both Blackpool and Morecambe were equal top of the league. The following week brought victory against Darwen and when Hilton bowled the West Indian Darwen professional Oliver Demming he had claimed his 100th league wicket of the season. With two games to go Morecambe beat Fleetwood and Netherfield beat Blackpool by the small margin of two runs meaning only a draw in the last match against Leyland Motors would be sufficient to bring the championship trophy to Woodhill Lane. A sub standard performance against Motors resulted in defeat and the champagne was left on ice until the news came through that Blackpool had also lost their last fixture enabling Morecambe to be crowned champions for the first time in the league's history.

A remarkable season had seen one of the basement clubs for many seasons win the league and cup double. Colin Hilton broke the league bowling record by taking an aggregate of 113 league wickets, a record still intact today. He was well supported by Ken Beal who took 28 wickets and Ray Jagger. Hilton's partner in many of those dismissals was wicketkeeper Roger Wrightson whose 518 runs made him the club's highest run scorer. Other run contributors were Graham Robinson, Charlie Clough, Frank Wilkinson, and Hilton himself.

In February 130 members and friends attended the Annual Dinner at the King's Arms Hotel to celebrate the clubs success. The Mayor Mr. WH Burgess addressed the meeting and said he hoped the cricket club would find a public benefactor that would come forward and enable the purchase of the ground for the sole use of cricket. He added that he thought the club would be fortunate to get a ground of their own but hoped the Education Authority would look favorably on them. The town's people expected trophies from the football team and the cricket team's success the previous season must have given an immense pleasure to the loyal band of members and supporters. Hoping the club would be rewarded with bigger gates he congratulated Colin Hilton on his record breaking 117 wickets, a record he thought would not be broken for a long time.

In reply Chairman Paul Speak said the club had taken more spectators to away games than any other team. Club President Laurie Boyden presented the ball mounted with which Colin Hilton took his 100th wicket in his record breaking season. League trophies were then presented to team members and tankards were presented to officials of the club. Roger Wrightson who could not attend due to heavy snow in the Whitehaven area was to receive the Ronson award for the wicketkeeper with the most victims in a season. This award was confined to the local cricketing leagues and clubs. Wrightson had come out on top with 28 victims.

Roger Wrightson had played Second XI cricket for Essex from 1959 and in 1965 he made his first-class debut against Oxford University. After playing a further nine County Championship games that year he did not make any appearances in 1966 and played just two games in 1967 after which he left the Essex county staff. In 1964 Wrightson played a few games in the County 2nd XI with Colin Hilton although this was not in the capacity as a wicketkeeper. Originally from Elsecar in Yorkshire he then moved back up north to West Cumbria and played a major part in the club's first championship success.

1968 was to be the only season Wrightson played and on joining Whitehaven he became one of their leading batsman. At this point he was selected for Minor Counties cricket with Cumberland and scored a century in his first game against the Yorkshire second team. Further appearances in 1971 were followed by a break as he went teaching in the West Indies for two years. Resuming playing on his return he was elected club captain at Whitehaven in 1980 and within a year had led them to the North Lancashire League Championship. Tragically in 1986 he died of a heart attack.

The AGM reported a profit of £500 on the previous season. Treasurer Roy Killip said that the football competition remained the main income for the club going up £200 to £457. Gate money had gone up from £30 to £125. In addition the club had taken a gate of £68 from the Slater Cup final and £13 from the semi final. Catering takings soared from £102 to £350 and the club also received an £85 donation from the Constitutional Club. Wages had increased £97 to £436. Although the finances of the club looked healthy the meeting was reminded that there was still no response from the Education Authority over plans to purchase the ground.

At the start of the 1969 season a reality check came with two defeats in the first two games against Fleetwood and then Preston with Mike Staziker as professional taking 3-28. The first win came the following week against Leyland Motors with scores of 190-6 declared (Charlie Clough making 86 and newcomer Bob Meadows 70 not out) to the visitors' reply of 58, Colin Hilton taking 7-27. Alan Evans was keeping wicket in the absence of Roger Wrightson and the consistency of the previous season was missing and Morecambe were always off from the leaders.

1969 will be remembered for a remarkable weekend in August however when Colin Hilton took 19 wickets in two games against Lancaster and Kendal. Hilton's analysis against Lancaster on the Saturday was 14.6 overs, 4 maidens, 34 runs and 10 wickets. All but one of his victims was bowled with only Lancaster professional Derek Parker standing firm on 13 not out.
Lancaster were all out for 78. Against Kendal on the Sunday

Morecambe batted first making just 124. With the ball Hilton carried on, where he left off, with a wicket first ball. At one point Kendal were 35-7 when Australian professional Roy Emerson and former Northamptonshire and Derbyshire
all rounder Michael Allen staged a mini recovery before the Kendal side subsided to 78 all out. Top scorer Allen was the wicket to escape Hilton's net as Ray Jagger had him caught by Harry Clarkson.

Hilton's net haul for the 1969 season was 88 wickets but with Ray Jagger next on 21 wickets there was a lack of support. Charlie Clough headed up the batting with Bob Mashiter and Alan Evans.

From the relatively stable financial position from the success of the previous season members were informed of a profit of just £41 from the 1969 season. Treasurer Roy Killip gave a warning saying: *"How long we can go I do not know?"* This was in relation to the fact that expenses had gone up by £228 while there was a drop in gate receipts to £77. Football club tickets were down over £100 and catering down as well. The professional's wages amounted to £287 and although the club had £760 in the bank this trend was to beset the club major financial issues in the years to come.

Colin Hilton was re-signed for the 1970 season but from Christmas onwards he had been ill and at the start of the season it was envisaged he would miss the first three or four weeks. Paul Gooch, Ken Goodwin and David Bailey all from the Lancashire Groundstaff acted as sub-pros in the first few weeks. Bailey was particularly successful scoring 109 in the victory against Kendal on the Saturday over Whitsuntide weekend. On the Monday Hilton made his first appearance in the return game but Morecambe were heavily defeated, 134 v 34. It was evident Hilton was short of fitness and match practice which clearly affected both his and ultimately the team's performance.

After a heavy defeat by Blackpool for whom West Indian Charlie Stayers was now the clubs professional, *'The Visitors'* Randall Butt gave a scathing report on the teams performance:

'It is difficult to see how Morecambe can ever win a match unless their game improves in every department and unless some remarkable metamorphosis takes place before Saturday the derby match against league pace setters Lancaster will be a massacre unsuitable for children or anyone of a nervous disposition.'

Maybe a little dramatic but for the first 30 minutes of the Lancaster game Morecambe lost three wickets without scoring a run and those words seemed appropriate. A recovery then ensued to take the total to a respectable 160 and a drawn game with the opposition finishing on 124-8. In July the club were at the bottom of the league and it was announced Colin Hilton would not be retained. A mini revival then took place with victories over Netherfield, Darwen, and Leyland with Hilton returning to form. In the last game of the season a defeat against St Anne's with scores of 90 v 69 and Colin Hilton's last game in which he bowled just three overs before retiring with an injured shoulder. Colin Hilton's current employment had come to an end and the following season he was engaged as professional for Walkden in the Bolton League. Hilton had taken 44 wickets while bowling only 150 overs. Alan Evans had been an able substitute behind the wickets taking 19 catches but the side had missed Roger Wrightson's batting if not his wicket-keeping.

On a more positive note the Reverend Jeff Yates took 60 wickets for the second team only three short of the club record held by Jack Simpson in 1960.

Chapter Nine— Black Days

Captain for the last three seasons, Charlie Clough declined the skipper's job for the 1971 season following which Frank Wilkinson was elected to the position at the club's AGM in February. Much of the talk at the meeting was about the composition of the committee and lack of work by some of the local councilors who had been associated with the club's committee over the last five years.

Come April, the club was to start the season with a new professional Mike Staziker who had completed a previous engagement at Preston in 1969 before embarking on a one-year contract at Lancashire in 1970. Staziker's county career was limited to just two County Championship appearances and just one solitary wicket. Staziker stayed just one year at Morecambe before moving on to play for Lancaster in an amazing 14 years of unprecedented success. Early indications of Staziker's ability to score runs came with his 74 not out against another of his former clubs, Leyland Motors.

It was another disappointing season for the first team finishing bottom of the league although they did manage four wins. The maverick journalist for 'The Visitor' Randall Butt was still entertaining readers with his individual style of reporting. One report included the following after a defeat by Blackpool.

'Bob Mashiter kept his cool, but Neville Manton drafted in from the 2nd team clearly had little time left at the crease. His style was as flamboyant as scorer Brian Pratt's shirt and tie combination, and after flailing his way to 5 runs he had his wickets shattered by the second ball of Laycock's over'.

On the 19th June the 2nd team registered their first win against Chorley by the small margin of five runs. In the Chorley team that day were two future internationals for England in the sports of Rugby Union and Football. Those players were Bill Beaumont and Paul Mariner.

Victory on the 7th August against Leyland Motors was the first of only four victories as the club had a strong run in towards the end of the season and Mike Staziker's form improved.

Staziker scored 444 runs and took 45 wickets at an average of just over 20 runs apiece. This was a poor performance in comparison to his 60 wickets in 1969 while playing for Preston at an average of less than 10 runs each.

Morecambe CC 1st X1 1972

Back Row L to R, R.H. Tattersall (Pro), J. Pirt, W. Bland, I. Perkin, N. Manton, A. Daniels, R. Jagger,

Front R. Mashiter, C. Clough, F. Wilkinson, R. Sandham.

In March 1972 the club put forward the idea of forming an Under 16 team to join the local youth league. President Laurie Boyden said he would donate a cup to the league if the club could get a team together. Bob Mashiter talked of a growing band of young cricketers attending on a Thursday night who had expressed an interest in forming a team. Problems may be with transport and equipment but he thought they could surely be overcome. He added that he would take responsibility with Roger Sandham helping out. Charlie Clough was re-elected as captain for the forthcoming season but once again it was reported that an unsuccessful bid to play at the Trimpell club meant the club was still looking for adequate playing facilities appropriate to a Northern League club. A loss of £135 on the previous season had been the result of higher ground expenses and poor gate receipts.

Roger Hartley Tattersall from the Lancashire groundstaff was signed as professional for the 1972 season. Tattersall had experience with Nelson in the Lancashire League as an 18 year old and had made just two

County Championship appearances for the Red Rose county. Throughout the season he made regular appearances for the county's 2nd X1 but never produced any form of note and a bottom of the table finish again ensued with just one win against Leyland. With only Ray Jagger included in the league's averages this showed a measure of some inept performances. The second team faired better with five wins and a century from Fred Normanton being the highlight of the season while finishing fourth from the bottom of Division Two.

The new junior section had however a successful season with at times up to 30 youngsters at practice nights. Throughout the winter negotiations with the Lancaster and Morecambe College of Further Education about use of their pitch took place but again this proved unsuccessful. The AGM reported a loss on the season of £150 with expenditure up by £300 due mainly to a new mower. The football clubs raffle had again been the saviour, raising £800.

In March 'The Visitor' reported and pictured a winter of vandalism at the club with the following words as the start of the season was only just around the corner.

'The evocative sound of leather on willow has been replaced by the rather less romantic one of brick on glass and splintering wood as more moronic elements of the community have taken their perverted pleasure at the other's expense'

Prior to the 1973 season the club received a further blow when Ray Jagger announced he would be leaving the area for business reasons and would not be available. Jeff Yates was the new captain and Colin Hilton returned as professional in the hope of returning to the glory year of 1968. Hilton started well enough with an 8-28 return against Netherfield but only four victories resulted in a second to the bottom of the table finish for the first team. Hilton's haul of 54 wickets was the fourth highest in the league and an excellent return considering the lack of support he received. The second team faired even worse finishing bottom of the league without a win.

If performances on the pitch were at near rock bottom then another blow for the club was the prospect of losing the ground. *The Visitor* reported due to the closure of Euston Road Secondary School the cricket field and surrounding fields had little use for the Education Authority and the County were considering the building of houses. The paper reported the club was on a year-to-year lease and any form of security for the club was clearly non-existent. Much debate on this subject was

Morecambe CC 1St X1 1974

Back Row Left to Right Rev. J.T. Yates, K. Beal, A. Daniels, R. Jagger, I. Hanson, C. Clough, Front R. Mashiter, J. Pirt, R. Sandham, A. Robinson (Pro), F. Wilkinson

brought up at the club's AGM in March were the Reverend Jeff Yates suggested the club should seek help from the newly formed District Council. Vandalism had again been prominent in the winter months but despite this the club had made a profit of £181. Roger Sandham was duly elected as captain for the forthcoming 1974 season and a new professional Adrian Robinson from Preston was signed by the club.

Robinson had previous experience with Oxford University, playing in the 1971 Varsity match at Lord's. Throughout the previous season he had played a number of games for the Lancashire Under-25 side. No doubt the club's finances were a major factor in him taking up his position at the club and his performances stood up to the change from amateur to professional. Another season of inept performances saw both the first and second teams manage just one win each while finishing at the foot of their respective league tables. Robinson and Bob Mashiter both scored over 450 runs each and Robinson was re-engaged for the following season but a crisis as big as the club was ever to face emerged in March 1975.

Since 1950 the club had paid £54 a year to the County Council for use of the Woodhill Lane ground from April to September. In late February the club was told the rent would be going up to £500. President Laurie Boyden had a personal meeting with a representative of the Council Estates Department and as a result the County's demand was reduced to £250 from April 1976, £275 the following year and £300 for the rest of a five-year lease. *"There is only one answer,"* said the President to *The Visitor. "We cannot afford it".* Vandalism had again been prevalent with sightscreens smashed, score box damaged, indoor toilets left in an appalling state and holes in the pavilion roof which needed repair. Financially the club could continue but a shortage of players had brought a situation that the club would not be able to field two teams.

Ray Jagger who had returned for part of the 1974 season, John Pirt, and the Rev Jeff Yates were due to leave the district before the start of the season, Ken Beal would not be available, and Bob Mashiter was leaving to play at Carnforth.

A special meeting was called prior to the club's AGM and members were urged to attend the meeting to be held at the Morecambe Hotel. A roll call produced just 12 seniors and two juniors as being available for the forthcoming season and the theme of the meeting evolved that poor facilities meant players would not come and play for the club. Losing five first team players from a team that finished bottom of the league meant that the club would not be able to compete in a league of Northern League's standard, commented one member. Secretary Billy Bland pointed out to the meeting the club might be asked to resign from the league because of the poor facilities. This situation had only just been averted before and was due to be reviewed prior to the forthcoming season. A proposal for the club to cease was put to the meeting at which Mr. Derek Mosey, Editor of *'The Visitor'* proposed an amendment for a fortnight's postponement, seconded by Mr. B Bichall. After the amendment was carried the club's AGM was also deferred for a fortnight.

Consultation with the County Education Authority by Derek Mosey about the possibility of buying a small piece of land on the ground for a new clubhouse, or alternatively a longer lease was discussed. Each option with a licensed bar had posed no objection and was reported back to members at the adjourned meeting. President Laurie Boyden said that all this was well but if they could not field two teams for the forthcoming season then all efforts would have been in vain.

A further roll call was taken and showed 25 players and two possibles.

Many of the clubs officials felt they could not carry on but Trevor Holgate put to the meeting a proposal that the club should carry on seconded by Neville Manton and this was carried. Preparations and repairs commenced in anticipation of the forthcoming season and a further plea for players was made in the local press.

Neither team managed to lift themselves off the foot of the table but there were more wins than the previous season by both sides and professional Adrian Robinson scored nearly 600 runs. A century against Leyland Motors at Woodhill Lane in one of the three league victories was an outstanding performance. This was to be Robinson's last of his two seasons at Woodhill Lane as he informed the club he would not be available for the following season due to a move to Kent in his employment with as a banker.

The patched up teams battled through the season with many performances than embedded the clubs never-say-die attitude. This was emphasized in a first team fixture away at Chorley. After the home side had batted first and scored heavily the wicket suddenly began to break up after the tea interval and John Butler, newcomer Keith Whittaker who had joined from local club Heysham, together with Jim Hetherington suffered blows to the face. Hetherington in particular suffered a broken nose leaving the field with blood cascading down his face with his score on 65 he then returned to the crease making 81 as the team finished 25 runs short of victory.

A season had been completed that in the previous March had seemed impossible and Derek Mosey had now taken over as Chairman of the club. There had developed a close association with the Morecambe and Heysham Constitutional Club and they had raised considerable funds for the club.

Derek Mosey had identified the derelict Scale Hall Railway Station as a building that had the potential to become the new clubhouse of Morecambe Cricket Club. Vice Chairman and builder Charlie Clough confirmed the building's structure was viable and the City Council stated that the building was the club's if they were able to remove the structure and clear the site. Club members young and old worked weekends to dismantle the wooden structure and transport the timber to Woodhill Lane. Plans were drawn up by Alan Birchall on how the existing structure could be adapted into the club's new pavilion and the Manpower Services Commission were approached and eventually agreed to build the new pavilion. Charlie Clough supervised the construction of the building and Derek Mosey swamped himself with

The old Scale Hall Railway Station that was transformed into the New Pavilion at Woodhill Lane.

the bureaucracy of negotiating with the County Council over a new lease on the Woodhill Lane ground.

In the shadow of the old pavilion the new building emerged and throughout the 1976 season visiting teams commented on the new development and applauded the club's vision and tenacity in making things happen.

New professional for 1976 was top order bat and occasional off spinner Colin Gradwell a seasoned player who had played for Lancashire 2nd XI in the early part of his career and was a vastly experienced league 'pro' who had experience in both the Central Lancashire League and the Bolton League. Colin Hilton returned to captain the side but his season was cut short as after the first four games injury prevented him taking any further part in the season. Gradwell scored over 500 runs with the retuning Tony Daniel and Roger Sandham, who had moved back to the club after one season at Lancaster figured in the league averages as the club finished third from the bottom of the first division.

President Laurie Boyden sadly did not live to see the new pavilion built as he died shortly after the initial work began. The President had seen the club through the success of 1968 and the basement finishes of the early seventies. But built it was and after the fine old pavilion had been constructed and opened in May 1900 this was now to succeeded by a new modern building that members hoped was to be the catalyst for a successful new era.

The 1977 season was another season that saw the club move forward with the evolving clubhouse and a side struggling to move away from a bottom four finish. Gradwell was retained as professional and Keith Whittaker started the season as skipper but the position had a number of incumbents before Tony Daniel completed the season as captain.

The new pavilion was officially opened in October 1977 by Laurie Boyden's son Kenneth and a memorial plaque unveiled in the new clubhouse in the memory of his father. The club became an instant magnet for many of the local residents living in close proximity of the Woodhill Lane ground and with volunteers from the clubs members manning the bar the social aspect was a huge success.

New professional for 1978 was Keith Barker, a West Indian based in the Blackburn area. Born in Barbados Barker had played for British Guiana before coming to England in 1965 for his first professional appointment in the Lancashire League at Enfield. A right arm fast medium bowler who batted in the middle order Barker played for number of clubs around the leagues and was well respected for his coaching. Previously at Great Harwood in the Ribblesdale League before his appointment at Morecambe Keith was well connected with all the leading West Indian cricketers of the time and a benefit game brought a host of star names to Woodhill Lane for his benefit game. A player who was involved in that game was a relatively unknown Australian who was the professional at East Lancashire Cricket Club in the Lancashire League. Alan Border played with a desire to win even though it was a benefit game and one memory was his ability to throw the ball from the furthest part of the ground straight into the wicket-keeper's gloves. Ironically he fielded the majority of his Test career close to the bat.

In 1978 a trend began in bringing young players from overseas in addition to a club's regular professional and Morecambe were indeed at the forefront of this initiative.

Don Mosey broadcaster, journalist and brother to the Morecambe chairman had many contacts around the cricketing world and none more so than in New Zealand were two young players whose fathers had been prominent figures in the development of New Zealand cricket set off on the long journey to Morecambe to gain a valuable cricketing experience.

First to arrive was Richard Reid son of former New Zealand Test captain John Reid. Reid was a nineteen year right hand batsman about to embark on a first-class cricket career with Wellington. Already established in the Wellington side was Robert Vance who arrived shortly after Reid and was an instant success in the Northern League. Vance's father had also had a successful career with Wellington.

Rob Vance was a hard hitting batsmen who immediately scored runs in quantity with scores of 83*,74, and 60* and Reid was also beginning to find his feet when both were enticed away from the club by Bradford League clubs offering a substantial remuneration for their playing services. Both players went on to represent their country. Reid played in nine One Day Internationals, his first in the 1987/88 season against England and then later in '90/91 for the World Series Finals in Australia. Reid played some outstanding cricket for Wellington when opening the batting with Martin Crowe. At 42 Reid was the appointed the Chief Executive at Canterbury after moving into Marketing with Nike after his playing career ended. Vance became a stalwart of the Wellington side making 199 appearances scoring 6,440 runs. International recognition came late at the age of 33 when he to was picked to play against England in 1987/88. A further three Tests followed against Pakistan (twice) and Australia in addition to eight one day internationals. Vance also holds the most unusual record of having the most runs scored off one of his overs in first-class cricket. In a game against Canterbury near the end of the '89/90 season which was heading for a draw Vance proceeded to bowl a series of gentle full pitches from beyond the popping crease to allow a total of 77 runs to be taken from the over.

The legacy of that early influx of Kiwis saw another fourth from the bottom finish with professional Barker taking 57 wickets and scoring over 500 runs, enough to earn himself another contract for the following season. Ian Gray had captained the side after a spell away at local club Heysham and taking over for 1979 after returning to the club after a spell at Lancaster was Peter Lambert. Originally from Settle, Yorkshire Lambert had played his early cricket with his hometown club together with the former Yorkshire and England spinner Don Wilson. Although Barker scored nearly 500 runs again he failed to take any five- wicket hauls and again a fourth from the bottom finish ensued.

At the end of the season Ray Jagger finally called it a day (although he

Paul Handley batting in the shadow of the big wheel against Blackpool in 1980

did make one second team appearance in 1980). After making his debut in 1959 he took just short of 400 first team wickets up to 1974 complemented by 175 victims in his later years in the second team taking a career best 8-41 in 1970.

Lambert continued with the captaincy in 1980 and brought to the club Ken Moore from Lancaster, Dave Jolleys from Palace Shield side Caton, Lynden Davies from Blackpool, and local footballer Paul Handley. After the short stay of the Kiwis the previous season the club refrained from the overseas market. New professional was a promising right arm fast bowler Richard Brown. Brown hailed from the Stockport area but the step-up to professional proved a difficult one and he ended the season with just 36 wickets at an average of nearly 25 runs each.

Par for the course another fourth from the bottom finish but the side now looked to have a more competitive edge as the club moved into the 'eighties.

Chapter Ten— Green Shoots

1981 was a season which had a range of top class internationals in the Northern League with West Indians at the forefront: Leonard Baichin at Kendal, Collis King at Blackpool and Rohan Kanhai at St Annes. Accompanying them were future Test internationals David Boon, Netherfield and Mike Whitney, Fleetwood from Australia, with New Zealander Trevor Franklin at Lancaster.

The standard of the League had increased and Morecambe with a new captain in ex-Lancaster stalwart Malcolm Hall found it difficult produce the form of the previous seasons and a bottom of the league finish ensued. Engaged as professional was fast bowler David Halliwell, well known throughout the league for his time as both an amateur and professional previously at Leyland. In 1975 Halliwell took 93 wickets to break his own Leyland record created the previous year. Halliwell had previous experience with Cheshire in the Minor Counties and in 1980 had been fulfilling the professional role at Colne in the Lancashire League. Halliwell scored 400 runs and took 65 wickets.

In the last game of the 1981 season away at Blackpool Malcolm Hall on performing the pre-match customary toss of the coin with the opposition captain Graham Fisher discussed the appropriate merits and performances of the closing season together with prospects for the following year. Fisher indicated he would be interested in playing at another venue by the seaside and consequently joined the club for the 1982 campaign. Fisher was to be a big part of Morecambe's future and he arrived at the club with an excellent track record of representative cricket. In 1975 at the age of 18 he had played for the MCC Schools team at Lords, England Young Cricketers, and also made his debut for the Lancashire 2nd XI. From 1976 to 1981 he continued to play for the county's 2nd XI while scoring heavily for Blackpool; indeed 1981 was his best season for Blackpool with 668 league runs.

Back at the club was Graham Robinson, part of the 1968 championship winning side who had moved to the Preston area after completing University to work as a schoolteacher. Robinson had been professional at Leyland Motors for the previous three seasons and had also played for Leyland as an amateur.

After Morecambe's venture into the overseas amateur market for Reid and Vance in the seventies the club had refrained due to the lack of security with such players. The League had now stipulated only one per club was allowed and again the club dipped its toe in the ocean by bringing another New Zealander to the club. Richard Brazendale was a right hand bat and slow left arm bowler from Auckland who made a useful if unspectacular contribution to the team.

Fisher was top of the clubs batting averages and Dave Jolleys the bowling as both first and second teams finished mid-table in 1982. What was clear for all to see was that both teams competing in a league that was enhancing its reputation for good cricket. The stature of the club grew in the early 'eighties with a thriving social side which resulted in the club extending the clubhouse to accommodate the increasing number of social members. From the outset the club's bar had been manned by volunteers from within the membership and it was not long before a steward to manage the bar was recruited. The playing surface was regarded as one of reliability as opposed to some of the cabbage patch wickets of years gone by and the financial worries of previous years had evaporated giving the club optimism for a bright future.

David Halliwell took 187 wickets in a three year period as professional at the club and after being released by the club took up the paid job at Kendal for the next three years. From 1981 to 1990 Halliwell had a successful engagement with Cumberland in the Minor Counties Championship reserving some of his best performances for the Nat West Trophy games. During the early 'eighties the developing club attracted further players and these included Keith Riley a wicket keeper from Oxfordshire, Neil Marsdin a slow left arm bowler, Geoff Bates who had played for Lancaster in that memorable game when Colin Hilton had taken all ten wickets, and Stuart Smith who had taken up employment in the area as a schoolteacher.

Ian Burnett a young fast bowler from Victoria, Australia played for the club as the overseas amateur in 1983. Burnett had played for Australian Universities against the England tourists on the 1979/80 tour claiming the wickets of Boycott, Willey, and Gooch in a drawn game. Burnett went on to take 44 wickets as the first team finished fourth in the table, the highest finish since 1968.

Graham Robinson scored 690 runs in the 1983 season breaking the previous record held by the late Ken Brooksbank.

The club had strength in depth and the second team took their first league trophy as runners up to Lancaster. The second team had seen little success in the league since the inception of the Northern League

Ravi Shastri on Woodhill Lane

but a mixture of youth and experience had brought the runners-up trophy to Woodhill Lane.

For the 1984 season the club enlisted the services of Indian Test player Ravi Shastri and appointed Graham Robinson as captain. The last overseas professional to play for the club was Australian Harry Lambert in 1951 and such a high profile signing in Shastri seemed a long way from the turmoil the club had endured ten years ago.

Ravi Shastri was already a stalwart of 27 Test matches and 21 One Day Internationals when he arrived in time for the start of the season as players, members and supporters awaited with high expectations of the Indian international. Shastri was 22 years old and had started his international career playing for and captaining the national Under 19 side. After a late call up to the national team touring New Zealand in '80/81 replacing the injured Dilip Doshi he took 15 wickets, the highest in the series and was named Man of the Match for the third Test in which he took seven wickets. Within 18 months of that Test series he had moved from tenth in the batting order to opening the innings. The failure of India's regular openers on the tour of England in 1982 resulted in him opening at the Oval. Not selected for the most

Back Row Left to Right : J. Butler, G. Fisher, R. Shastri, B. Arun, G. Bates, R. Bywater, Front Row L to R: D. Twynham, I. Fisher, S. Smith, A Speak, K. Riley.

important matches of the 1983 World Cup he then distinguished himself with gutsy performances against the domineering West Indian pace bowlers and then arrived at Morecambe for the 1984 season.

First game of the season was against Fleetwood at Woodhill Lane but Tommy Scott, Jack Armstrong, Steve Lawton and John Wright upset the party winning by five wickets, Morecambe 144 all out Fleetwood 145-5. Shastri took the five wickets to fall and if evidence was needed that international professionals did not bring instant success a dour losing draw against Kendal and a ten wickets defeat against Blackpool showed everybody that application even from the highest order was required.

The standard of the league was as competitive as it had ever been and with nearly all clubs having the services of an overseas amateur Morecambe were at a disadvantage. Talks with Shastri resulted in a young fast bowler to come over from India for his first experience of English conditions. 18 year old Chetan Sharma had represented his country in four One Day Internationals and completed his first full season for Haryana and North Zone in the Indian domestic season.

On Whit Monday against Lancaster Shastri guided the side to victory by just one wicket but as the season arrived at the halfway point just three victories had been recorded. An indifferent season continued and resulted in a mid table finish. Shastri took 60 wickets and scored 650 runs. Sharma took 44 wickets and showed enough to indicate he would have a successful career which indeed he went on to achieve. Chetan Sharma made up for a lack of height and build with a quick whippy action that surprised many batsman with the pace he could generate although many experts said he would not last long in international cricket. To a certain degree he disproved that theory by playing 23 Test matches and 65 One Day Internationals. After playing for Morecambe as an amateur in 1984 he returned to England in 1986 with India to take 16 wickets in two Tests and become the first Indian bowler to take ten wickets in a Test in this country.

While all the focus was on the first team the second team under the leadership of Colin Wilson played out a close fought Blackledge Trophy Final against St Annes which resulted in the second team winning by just nine runs.

The club entered negotiations to resign Shastri for the following season and successfully gained a commitment from the Indian international to return. Return he did but in the intervening winter period he played in the Test series against Pakistan his third in six years, and then England against who he scored 142 in the Bombay Test followed by 111 at Calcutta. In January between the Test Matches and One Day Internationals Shastri played for Bombay against Baroda in a Ranji Trophy match in which he became one of the elite cricketers to hit six sixes in an over, the unfortunate bowler being left arm spinner Tilak Raj. In February and March in the Benson and Hedges World Championship of Cricket tournament in Australia Shastri's performances earned him the Man of the Series award and a new Audi 100 car. The Indian Prime Minister Rajiv Gandhi instructed the Indian customs to waive the heavy duty its import would normally have entailed. Through the advent of satellite television many of his previous year's acquaintances in the Northern League viewed the competition which increased Shastri's standing as one of the worlds leading all rounders.

This was the first time overseas cricket matches had been shown live in India and Shastri had now become a world cricketing icon. While club members watched and read about the exploits of Shastri the clubhouse

Ravi Shastri and former overseas player Ian Burnett pictured at the club in 1985

continued to be a social hub of the local community and a planning application to extend the clubhouse was approved by the local council.

At the start of the 1985 season Shastri arrived late and a future England International in Yorkshire's Paul Jarvis arrived to sub-pro in the first game against Kendal and took a five wicket haul in a drawn game. Stuart Smith had taken over the reins as skipper as Graham Robinson left to play at Preston. A remarkable season in which Morecambe drew 15 games resulted in a third place finish behind runners up Leyland and champions Fleetwood for whom West Indian pace bowler Franklyn Stephenson took 94 wickets. This was the club's highest league finish since 1968. From just 16 innings Shastri scored 840 runs to break the club's professional batting record set by Jack Parker in 1953 and delighted the spectators around the league grounds with some awesome batting performances. None more so than when he scored 136 not out at Preston where, with boundaries set to the edge of the enormous playing area, he had two all-run fives in Morecambe's

Graham Fisher and Martin Pickles in front of the Scorebox showing
the record breaking opening partnership

total of 255-2. Shastri's bowling that year captured 52 wickets. In
between his weekend commitments Shastri traveled the length and
breadth of the country visiting fellow countrymen on the league and
county circuit, he played in various Testimonials and Benefit games,
while still finding time to attend some of the more traditional English
summer institutions such as Wimbledon.

Once again the club used Shastri's knowledge to bring over an overseas
player. Playing for the club in 1985 was Bharathi Arun, a stocky built
all rounder who bowled at brisk medium pace and batted in the middle
order. Arun had been part of the Indian Under 19 side that toured Sri
Lanka in 1979 under the captaincy of Shastri and went on to play two
Tests against Sri Lanka in the 86/87 season. Both players left early,
Arun due to commitments with domestic cricket and Shastri to tour Sri
Lanka with India at the end of August. Filling this void at the end of
the season was a young West Indian Phil Simmons who went on to play
international cricket and former New Zealand captain Geoff Howarth
whose reign at Surrey was to finish that season.

With Shastri now recognized as one of the world's best all rounders the
club reluctantly resigned itself to the fact there would be no return and
indeed Shastri went on to play for Glamorgan from 1987 to 1991. The
club was left with memories of an individual who found it easy to mix

Chetan Sharma, India
Morecambe CC Professional, 1987

and socialize with all the members, playing his cricket with the utmost respect for his teammates and opponents, and recognition that the two overseas amateurs he had brought to the club went on to represent their country at the highest level.

During the 1985 season chairman Charlie Clough announced that the Woodhill Lane ground now belonged to the club once again after concluding the purchase of the ground from Lancashire County Council for £60,000. Since 1922 officials had tried to bring the ground back into ownership of the club but to no avail. The Council had originally requested £150k but negotiations had reduced the figure to the final purchase price which was to be paid for by a Sports Council grant of £15k, the club's own £25k Development fund, an interest free loan of £10k from the Bass Brewery, and the rest from a bank loan. This however had implications on the proposed extension that had to be put on hold as purchase of the ground was priority.

In looking for a replacement for 1986 the club turned to Roger Brown, a right arm fast bowler from Tasmania. Brown took 67 wickets with seven five- wicket plus performances and on several occasions bowled with real pace. Joining the club that year was Martin Pickles from Blackpool. Pickles opened the batting with Fisher and scored nearly 600 runs. Fisher continued to gather in the runs scoring 820 which included four centuries and a top score of 149 not out. Fisher and Pickles put on a club record opening partnership of against St Annes; this however was not enough to secure victory as the game petered out into a draw. A fourth from the bottom finish did not represent the potential of the side.

Chetan Sharma fresh from his exploits with the Indian national team returned as the club's professional for the 1987 season and Stuart Smith's captaincy brought out the best in the side. Smith and a youthful Phil Thornton both scored useful runs complimenting Fisher and Pickles. In the bowling department Neil Marsdin, Ian Ledward, and John Butler all took 20 plus wickets while Sharma scored 480 runs and took 45 wickets. All this brought about a resurgent team that was involved in the tightest finish the league had seen when on the last Saturday of the season any one of five teams could win the league.

Prior to that, however, the side had reached the final of the Matthew Brown Cup after beating Darwen in the first round and Preston in the semi-final. The final against Leyland at Fox Lane was a disappointment as Morecambe could only make 90 and proceeded to lose by seven wickets. Another successful cup run in the 'Cockspur Cup' the club reached the Regional semi final and a home fixture against Read from the Ribblesdale League who included Burnley and Wales soccer international Leighton James. A disappointing performance saw the home team lose by 12 runs. Few people would have thought that day that Leighton James would not only return to play cricket for Morecambe and manage the town's football club.

Back to the final Saturday of that season and Morecambe had had to field sub professional Indian pace bowler Atul Wassan for the run-in to the end of the season as Chetan Sharma had been called back to India in preparation for the Deodhar Trophy competition with North Zone.

Lancaster, Leyland, Fleetwood and Darwen back in fifth place were the other clubs involved as a poor day weather wise resulted in some shortened games. Morecambe, losing the toss against Darwen were asked to bat first and could only score 121. It was not enough as

Darwen ran out winners and other results meant level points at the top of the league between the Birch Hall team and Leyland. A play-off took place and Darwen, coming from fifth place, defeated Leyland to win the title.

1988 saw the recruitment of another Indian Test player in Gopal Sharma, a diminutive off-spinner who could turn the ball vast amounts. Sharma's consistent performances kept the team in contention within a league whose reputation was enhanced by Preston and Blackpool's recruitment of Pakistan legend Javed Miandad and Indian left arm spinner Maninder Singh respectively. Blackpool with Martin Pickles returning did indeed win the league with Preston runners-up. Joining the club from North Lancashire League side Carnforth was Gulam Maje who had a successful first season taking 41 league wickets and a youthful Peter Stephens made his entrance into Northern League cricket playing for the second eleven, who had a successful season, finishing runners up in the league and Latus Trophy finalists.

Two cup competitions were introduced in 1988 and both were won by Preston but not without controversy. In the Matthew Brown Trophy semi-final at West Cliff Preston playing Morecambe were dismissed for 92 with Ian Ledward taking the prize wicket of Miandad and John Butler taking four wickets. Steady progress was made by Morecambe's batsmen as storm clouds gathered. A heavy downpour then ensued forcing the players from the field. After a couple of hours delay the sun and a drying wind allowed the umpires to consider the pitch fit for play at which point the Preston team proceeded to bowl just fourteen deliveries in 26 minutes. Under immense pressure and with the light deteriorating the umpires took the players from the field adjudging that insufficient time was available to conclude the game. A replayed game the following week resulted in a Preston victory.

Gopal Sharma was retained for the following season and the side looked to build on a mid-table position. Stuart Smith again led from the front scoring over 600 runs which was just behind Graham Fisher's 677. Sharma who contributed nearly 400 runs and 47 wickets was supported in the bowling department by Stephens, Maje, and Butler. Despite these performances the side finished fourth from the bottom with just four wins and the cup competitions offered little comfort with two defeats against local rivals Lancaster. The second eleven faired better with a joint third place finish in the league, but replicated the first team's form in the cups with two defeats against Lancaster.

A generally disappointing season was suddenly brightened in mid

Slalom Lager Trophy winning side
1990 at the old Leyland Motors ground.
Back Row: Brian Paton, Keith Riley, Craig Atkins, Rashid Patel, Brewery Representative, Colin Knight, Jeff Stobbart, Mark Armistead, Ian Hanson, Paul Speak,
Front Row: Ian Ledward, Graham Fisher, Phil Thornton, Michael Lamb, Gulam Maje, Stuart Smith.

season when Sharma was ill and sub professional Robert Haynes was brought in from Lancashire League club Accrington. West Indian Haynes was from Jamaica and immediately made an impact in the game against Preston for whom New Zealand Test batsman Mark Greatbatch and former England player Graham Roope were in opposition. Batting first Haynes proceeded to hit the ball to all parts of the huge playing area at West Cliff scoring 126 not out and Graham Fisher making 102 not out in a total of 265-1. Playing his full part in the game Haynes then took the ball bowling brisk medium pace followed by leg spin in taking 3-65 from 24 overs as Preston successfully negotiated a draw. With Sharma missing for the next game again Haynes substituted and repeated his previous week's performance scoring 138 hitting seven sixes and fifteen fours in a closely drawn game against Kendal. Haynes had showed his class and his impact in the two games reverberated around the league. Little were club players and officials who reveled in his performances able to foresee the events prior to the 1991 season which enabled him to join the club.

Gopal Sharma was not retained for the 1990 season and club officials led the search for a suitable replacement. South African all-rounder Neville Daniels was signed and prospects looked positive when it was announced there were to be two new arrivals at the club. Just a few weeks before the start of the season Daniels pulled out with injury and a frantic search for a replacement resulted in Indian Rashid Patel signing for the club. Patel had played one Test and one ODI for his country in 1988 against New Zealand. Patel scored an early season fifty but this was a false dawn as his batting disappointed. With the ball Patel bowled quickly but his direction was poor and he returned just 31 league wickets in the season.

The two newcomers both came from North Lancashire League clubs. Colin Knight, a hard hitting opening batsman from Lindal Moor had a hugely successful season breaking the club's amateur batting record scoring 783 runs, just one more than Graham Fisher's 782 in 1986. His score of 154 against Preston was the club's highest and the league's highest individual score in the Northern League. Knight and Fisher's opening partnership was regarded as the best in the league and was more than emphasized in the ten wickets defeat of Kendal. In reply to the Cumbrians' 170-9 Knight 74 not out and Fisher 85 not out secured victory without loss.

Knight's stay was all to brief as he returned back to Lindal Moor for the following season. Australian Craig Atkins was the other new recruit. Residing on the Furness peninsula, he had played for a number of clubs in that area before being enticed to play for Morecambe in the Northern League. Atkins broke the club's amateur record taking 63 wickets at just 12.87 runs apiece and finished top of the league bowling averages. Such a performance put him in the market and it was no surprise when Lancaster signed the slow left arm bowler as professional for the 1991 season and indeed the following three seasons. During this period he qualified to play County cricket and in 1994 after playing some 2nd XI fixtures for Northamptonshire, Essex, Leicestershire he signed for Northamptonshire. Atkins failed to make the grade and played just one first class game as Northants' overseas player Anil Kumble took 105 wickets.

With such calibre of players a highly successful season ensued with a fourth place finish in the league and the side reaching both finals of the cup competitions. In the Slalom Lager Trophy final in the first half of the season a victory against Leyland Motors at Sandy Lane was followed by Kendal winning the second final, the Matthew Brown Trophy at Woodhill Lane.

1990 was a particularly successful season for Mark Armistead taking 70 second team wickets to surpass Jack Simpson's record that had stood for 30 years.

Colin Knight stayed just the one season before returning to the North Lancashire League and with Atkins moving across the Lune the prospects for the 1991 season did not appear particularly bright. With the news in February that no still no professional had yet been engaged events took a dramatic turn when it was revealed that Jamaican Robert Haynes who had successfully acted as sub professional for the club in two games in 1989 could not agree terms with his Lancashire League club Accrington and was available. Haynes had played for Accrington in both 1989 and 1990. In both seasons the club was runners-up in the Lancashire League with Haynes contributing nearly 947 runs and taking 109 wickets in 1989 and scoring 694 runs and 90 wickets in 1990. The club moved swiftly and secured a signed contract for the forthcoming season.

Chapter Eleven — Hitting The Heights

The first game of the 1991 season had Haynes missing due to flight problems and Lancashire's Gary Yates stood in scoring 59 in the victory against Fleetwood, and another newcomer Damian Gudgeon from Lancaster scored 30 not out. Haynes hit three centuries in accumulating 690 league runs for the season and took 50 wickets. Support from Graham Fisher with 760 runs was all in vain with as a mid-table finish ensued. Morecambe were trying to keep pace with teams of a high pedigree such as League Champions Leyland who had a catalogue of stars with New Zealander Mark Greatbatch, former Derbyshire and England off spinner Geoff Miller, ex Morecambe pro David Halliwell and England Youth captain Gary Wells in their ranks. Blackpool had West Indian Test batsmen Richie Richardson, and just to show the strength of the amateurs in the league Kendal reached the final of the 'Cockspur' National Club Knock-out.

The depth of playing strength within the club had developed and for the first time since the formation of the Northern League the 2nd XI under Kevin Demain secured the Second Division title. 1990 was a memorable season for Mark Armistead as he bagged a record haul of 70 victims in becoming the club's 2nd XI leading wicket-taker. A prolific wicket taker at that level Armistead captured 531 wickets with a best of 9-33 in 1987. Second team captain Kevin Demain broke the club's 2nd division batting record with 637 runs in 1993 and then proceeded to go past that record in 1995, scoring 676 runs.

From 1980 Morecambe had entered a 3rd XI into The South Lakeland League followed by a 4th XI in 1984. There was no doubt that the formation of these teams allowed youngsters from a thriving junior section to progress through the ranks. The 3rd XI enjoyed First Division status for several years, senior players such as Peter Lambert, Colin Wilson and Ian Gray were the mainstays of an ever changing team.

In 1992 Robert Haynes had what many club members would consider his best season as his performances led a resurgent team to the league title, the first time since 1968. Winning the league by a single point from Chorley, Haynes scored 931 runs including two centuries and took 72 wickets. Haynes broke the clubs professional batting aggregate held by Ravi Shastri from 1985. He was supported by skipper Graham Fisher with 523 runs and tidy bowling from Peter Stephens and Gulam Maje. With Haynes playing such a domineering part in proceedings Mark Mace, former Lancaster player Dave Derham who had joined the

Graham Fisher and Robert Haynes with the
Northern League championship trophy in 1992

club from Settle, and Bill Rawstron from Haynes' old club Accrington, together with wicketkeeper Keith Riley, all played supporting roles.

The club's 2nd XI brought home more silverware from the Latus Trophy final at Windsor Park against Chorley who included Paul Grayson, a future England Rugby Union International in their ranks.

The club was prominent throughout the 'nineties in all competitions with all of its four senior teams. The list of silverware is a record of a successful period in the club's history when the club not only thrived on the field but established itself as part of the local community around Woodhill Lane. This was achieved by a hard working chairman and former player Ian Hanson with his committee and army of helpers who worked tirelessly to raise funds through the obligatory 'Sportsman's Dinner', Raffles, Match Ball Sponsors, and 'Mini Sportsman's Evenings' held at the club.

In 1993 the first team were runners up in the Theakstons Best Bitter Cup to a star studded Leyland team that included the legendary West Indian batsmen Gordon Greenidge. Faruk Patel who had progressed to first team cricket after his move from Lancaster produced an inspired spell of bowling to record the best figures in the league that season with 9-42 against Preston. The following year resulted in the runners-up trophy in both the Vaux Bitter Cup and the Vaux Samson Cup. To make up for the disappointment of the first team being pipped at the post in two cup finals, the second team won the League Championship and the Blackledge Trophy, narrowly missing out on the chance of a treble by losing to Preston who went on to win the trophy. The third team in the newly formed Northern League Division 3 won the league and the cup. Professional Haynes produced many all round performances and recalling just one occasion will give a flavour of his talent.

A rain affected game against Darwen at Woodhill Lane started late. Under the rules Darwen batting first would receive 30 overs while Morecambe batting second would receive 21. Darwen accumulated 126 and in reply Morecambe were well behind the run rate at the half way stage until Haynes entered at the fall of the second wicket. Progressing his way towards the oppositions score the requirement of 11 to win from two balls was required as the fielders were placed on the boundary edge. Haynes proceeded to smash both deliveries for six over the mid wicket boundary to the joy of the home spectators.

It was Darwen who gained revenge in the Vaux Final of 1994 which after being washed out on two occasions was played on the first Saturday after the conclusion of the season. This was unusual as both professionals had left for their domestic teams and both clubs were instructed to play without a professional.

Robert Haynes took 84 wickets in 1995 setting up the club for its third league championship since the league's inception. With an aggregate of 700 runs in addition in league games Haynes had become a wanted man. In stepped Radcliffe from the Central Lancashire League with an offer surpassing anything the club could compete with and Haynes duly signed. What followed was a disappointing season for Haynes as he failed to capture the form he had displayed on many occasions at Woodhill Lane and his tenure with the CLL team lasted just one season.

Robert Haynes played in eight One Day Internationals for the West Indies prior to signing for Morecambe. Unfortunately he did not display his domestic form for Jamaica on the international stage and after retiring from first-class cricket he coached Jamaica from 1999 to 2006. Winning the Carib Beer Cup in 2004/05 he quit the following season when the side finished bottom of the table but in 2008 he was recruited as a National Selector.

Robert Haynes in action at Woodhill Lane against Kendal

Searching for a new professional the club signed South African Steven Pope from the Border club for the 1996 season. Pre-season news was that Dave Derham had returned to Lancaster to captain the side and the club were looking for John Eccles to step up and be the club's main spin bowler. Pope duly arrived on time and the first game of the campaign was against Leyland Motors at Sandy Lane. Lancashire player Dexter Fitton who had re-written the record books for Carnforth in the North Lancashire League the previous season was sub professional for the Motors. Fitton proceded to smash the ball to all parts of the ground scoring 139 not out in a Leyland score of 216-7. In reply Morecambe could only muster 149-9 in the drawn game. Steven Pope gave little indication of what was to follow that season falling LBW to Fitton for a duck.

With no silverware in 1996 from the club's senior teams it could be regarded as a disappointment such was the expectancy after the Haynes era. Steven Pope did, however, become the first and only Morecambe batsmen to score over one thousand league runs in a season. Scoring 1,114 runs he overtook Robert Haynes record of 931 runs in 1992. Pope and Haynes had both been provided with a superb platform in which to score runs from on a Woodhill Lane square that was highly regarded throughout the league as a superb batting track. The club had invested in new machinery but the main credit was due to groundsman Jack Mason who provided a playing surface second to none.

In November the club launched a project to build a 'School of Excellence' in the confines of the Woodhill Lane ground. The building was to cost £1 million and a club appeal for £323,000 was launched. The scheme had the backing of the Lancaster City Council and it was hoped to attract Lottery funding for the rest of the total. The scheme was two fold in that it would also improve the pavilion facilities such as changing rooms, function room, and provide a new roof.

Again in 1997 the club's two senior teams hauled in the silverware with the first team being runners-up in the Vaux Samson Trophy and then winning the Vaux Bitter Cup, the second team winning the Latus Trophy. In the Vaux Bitter Semi Final Mark Woodhead scored a memorable 129 not out in the victory over Lancaster and the cup was only won after a tied first attempt against St Annes with the scores at Morecambe 144-8 and St Annes 144-6. In a more conclusive final Morecambe scored 251-3 and St Annes 174 all out, with Steve Pope leading the run charge with 93.

Pope failed to emulate his achievements of the previous season in the league scoring 692 runs, however this was enough to earn another contract and he duly returned in 1998 to score 989 runs. At the end of this season the club parted company with Pope and began the search for a new professional. The second team won the Latus Trophy for the second season in succession and completed a successful season by finishing runners-up in the league.

Steven Pope went onto to play league cricket in Cornwall for a number of years and represented his adopted county in the Cheltenham & Gloucester Trophy in 2001/2/3. After initially playing for the new franchise team the 'Warriors' he retired from first-class cricket in May 2005 but still managed to be coaxed into playing a few games for the Border team later in the following season.

In January 1999 the Western Province and future England coach Duncan Fletcher recommended a highly regarded young left hander to the club in Ashwell Prince. Beating off opposition from a Ribblesdale League club for his signature Prince arrived for the start of the season and proceeded to find his feet on the slow early season wickets. He scored 631 runs and he played a significant part in the team's success of 1999 in winning the Vaux Bitter Cup. Victories against Leyland DAF, Darwen, and Blackpool in the Semi Final paved the way for a final against Chorley at Woodhill Lane. Chorley were defeated by four wickets, Morecambe replying with 175-6 to Chorley's 171-6. It was, however, the semi-final against Blackpool which made all the headlines for the wrong reasons.

Discipline among the players in the league was of concern and had already been recorded in the league's handbook as an issue that needed addressing. Leaving the field from the first innings of the Blackpool side a previous incident resulting in the collision of two players escalated with Faruk Patel and David Bartholmew having an altercation which left Bartholmew requiring hospital treatment. A lengthy disciplinary process followed and Patel served a ban while the national and regional press looked to report the incident at every opportune moment.

In 1999 the 2nd XI won the Division Two championship winning 16 out of the 22 games played and losing just once.

In the Millennium year of 2000 the club retained Ashwell Prince as professional and although the club did not collect any silverware it made its one and only appearance in a Lancashire Cup semi-final losing to the eventual winners Netherfield. A call-up to the national team resulted in Prince returning home early and under the rules of the competition the club were not allowed to field a substitute. Prince's second season saw him scoring 559 runs from just 14 innings before his early departure.

Prince was a most popular professional and he left with a host of friends and acquaintances he remembers to this day. His success on the international stage is well known throughout the club's present fraternity and any opportunity for him to revisit the club is well received.

Throughout this most successful period in the clubs history there were many individual performances too numerous to list but some of the more influential players need recording just as Brooksbank, Youren, Thompson, and Williams have been in previous chapters of the book.

In 2000 Graham Fisher retired from the game after joining the club from Blackpool in 1982. A previous amateur club batting aggregate holder and former club captain he scored just short of 14,000 runs including ten centuries for both clubs with a top score of 149 not out in the record opening partnership with Martin Pickles in 1986 against St Annes at Woodhill Lane.

Two bowlers stepped up in the nineties. Gulam Maje joined the club from North Lancashire League club Carnforth in 1988 which proved to be his best season with the ball taking 41 wickets. A consistency then followed as he collected a regular supply of wickets while giving little away. Many would say he kept some of his best performances for the cup matches with array of frugal bowling figures. In 1988 Peter Stephens joined the club from Palace Shield side Torrisholme while he did indeed make his first first-team appearance in that year he adjusted to the step-up by collecting many second division victims while in the process overcoming a serious knee injury to firmly cement himself in the first team in 1996. An avalanche of first team wickets followed and in 2002 he helped himself to a club record 75 victims, overtaking the previous record held by Craig Atkins. Peter Stephens took a total of 815 Northern League wickets over his career including 500 wickets at first team level, the highest wicket taker in the club's history. Mark Woodhead made his first team bow in 1992 and four years later in 1996 had his best season scoring 682 league runs and in future years was to prove a solid reliable opening batsman.

Towards the end of the twentieth century Philip Thornton took over the reins as captain of the side. After restricted appearances through his employment and injury in the early 'nineties Thornton was, like Mark Woodhead a product of the club's juniors and South Lakeland teams in progressing to the club's first team. It is with no doubt that no other Morecambe player has been able to hit the ball as hard and as far as Thornton and for this reason he became a popular and respected ambassador for the club.

In 2001 Thornton broke the club's amateur batting record scoring a total of 871 runs in a season that also saw him score two centuries. In 2005 his performances were rewarded with his appointment as professional at Ribblesdale League club Whalley for just one season, returning to Morecambe in 2006.

Accompanying Thornton was a new professional in Amol Muzumdar an Indian batsmen from the Mumbai team who had previous league experience in the Bradford League for Windhill. A pre-season scare with regard to a discipline issue was unfounded and the Indian batsmen scored 817 runs in an accomplished manner that said much about his upbringing in playing with the legendary Sachin Tendulkar

Phil Thornton

and Vinod Kambli at school and youth level. A mid-table finish left the playing side on a stable footing as the club moved forward into the progressive twenty first century and the advent of coloured kit and 20/20 cricket.

The Northern League celebrated its 50th anniversary with a celebration dinner at the Blackpool Hilton in March prior to the start of the 2002 season. Members and visiting guests had the usual comforts of Woodhill Lane put on hold as the clubhouse was extended and uplifted. This activity was project managed by former first team captain Ian Gray and was a diluted version of 'The School of Excellence' scheme. The works concluded during the season and both club members and visiting teams took advantage of the improved facilities. Brian Close the ex-England, Yorkshire and Somerset player officially opened the new extension in October that year.

Club resources were stretched and this resulted in a reduced budget for the engagement of a professional who came in the form of Indian off spinner and hard hitting lower order batsman Ramesh Powar from the same Mumbai team as the club's previous professional Amol Muzumdar.

Powar had been professional at Ryton in the North East and needed a step- up in the standard of league cricket, hence his acceptance to join the club. Powar proved himself to be a major force within the league scoring 677 runs and taking 61 wickets. Phil Dennison, Tommy Clough, Mark Woodhead and Phil Thornton all made significant contributions with the bat as the side finished runners-up to league champions Darwen. Peter Stephens bowled himself into the clubs record books taking 75 wickets to surpass previous record holder Craig Atkins' amateur record. Morecambe's second place total of 215 points was a huge 44 points in front of third placed Netherfield. Powar left early as he was recalled by his Indian employers at Mumbai. This opened the way for another Indian Robin Morris to join the team for the August Bank Holiday fixture at Lune Road against Lancaster. Morris scored a magnificent 134 in the drawn game.

Another player making a guest appearance for the second eleven was Mark Halsey better known as a Premier League referee. Halsey made a few other appearances for the 4th XI under the watchful eye of Dave Allison. A multitude of players contributed to the second team winning the Division Two championship with Ian Izatt the major run contributor and Graham Lee and Jonathan Gates taking 98 wickets between them.

Ramesh Powar was back for the following season but failed to reproduce his superb form of the previous year scoring just short of 400 runs and taking just 34 wickets. Powar returned to India were he put in some consistent performances for the Mumbai side earning himself international recognition in the one day side as a typical bits and pieces player.

Once again runs were a plenty at Woodhill Lane but after another bag of 54 wickets from Stephens the bowling lacked support as the side finished in fifth place. Phil Dennison threatened the amateur batting record but finished 50 short with a total of 820 runs and the highlight of the season was a Thwaites Smooth Trophy final win against Netherfield.

After much searching for a suitable professional for the 2004 season, the club secured the signature of South African right arm fast medium bowler Charl Langeveldt. Langeveldt had been in England the previous season for the 'Nat West Bank' triangular series with Zimbabwe and England. In 2002 the South African had played just a few games at Colne in the Lancashire League before an ankle injury meant he had to return home early. Brendan Hetherington returned from Lancaster to keep wicket as early season expectations were dampened by the news the Langeveldt would be delayed. West Indian Test player Franklyn Rose was engaged as the sub professional and kept everybody entertained as the club made a winning start. Langeveldt duly arrived and made an instant impression scoring a half century in his first game at league newcomers Barrow but South African Lancaster professional Renier Munnik dented the early season form when on Whit Monday he took the Morecambe bowlers apart in scoring 160 with ten sixes and 13 fours out of a Lancaster total of 257-6. Morecambe were never in the chase and lost by 129 runs.

Langeveldt was bowling well and Morecambe were among the leading pack as the season moved into the second half. A visit to Woodhill Lane by eventual league winners Fleetwood resulted in the home team managing just 103. Not to be outdone Langeveldt excelled with 8-38 as Fleetwood could only manage 87. At the end of July against Leyland, Langeveldt scored a magnificent 156 and Gareth Pedder 56 out of a Morecambe score of 276-5 declared which is the highest Northern League score by the club. As the side prepared for the league run-in Langeveldt had received instructions to return home for 'A' team tour of Zimbabwe and following this the 'A' team tour to Sri Lanka. Performances dipped as sub-professionals were difficult to find and a fourth place finish finally ensued. The clubs 2nd XI won the league and cup double with Faruk Patel breaking the club and league second division bowling record by taking 81 wickets at an average of just 10.93 apiece.

2004 saw the introduction to the Northern League of the club's old North Lancashire League adversaries Barrow for whom the last league meeting was in 1946, although the clubs had met more recently in National KO cup competition. Moving away from the traditional form of league cricket the first 20/20 competition was held with Kendal being the first winners as increased attendances showed this form of cricket was popular.

In 2005 Phil Dennison took over the club captaincy from Phil Thornton and all-rounder Mark Orchard from the New Zealand state side Northern Districts was signed up as professional. Orchard had had previous experience with St Helens Recs in the Liverpool Competition be it the First Division as opposed to the superior Premier Division but had excelled with over 800 runs and 78 wickets. Dennison led from the front with 634 runs supported by Orchard with 720 and other contributions from Woodhead and Pedder. South African Malibongwe

Maketa came to work in the area and joined the club. Having previously played for South Africa Under 15's it did not take long for the potential of the newcomer to shine through in scoring over 550 runs in an all to brief one season stay at the club. The lack of bowling penetration caused most problems with Orchard taking 49 wickets; his nearest challenger was Gareth Pedder with 24. A mid-table finish was the end result and again the professional had to leave early. On August Bank Holiday against Lancaster Charl Langeveldt while enjoying a stint of county cricket with Somerset found time to deputise for Orchard taking 4-56 at Lune Road as the season folded with defeat against Darwen at Woodhill Lane. The club made attempts to resign Orchard for the following season but terms could not be agreed and in the end Orchard signed for East Lancs in the Lancashire League.

Phillip Thornton returned to the club for the following season from his brief professional engagement with Whalley in the Ribblesdale League and accompanying him was to be Mark Lomas who in 1999 had been professional at Blackburn Northern in the Ribblesdale League and played at Blackpool between 2000 and 2003 before returning to play for East Lancashire, a club at which he originally played his senior cricket. New professional for 2006 was South African Garnett Kruger a tall fast medium bowler who the previous winter had toured Australia playing in three one day internationals. Another newcomer was Vishal Goyal an Indian student at Lancaster University who had impressed in pre-season nets.

First game of the 2006 campaign was against Barrow and Mark Orchard now at East Lancs deputized for the late arrival of Kruger, taking four wickets as the side started with a victory under a new captain in Tommy Clough. This appointment did not last longer than the first five weekends as Lomas took over the captaincy and the team shaped up for a championship charge. Early leaders were Lancaster but despite a defeat on the Saturday of Whitsuntide weekend to St Annes, Morecambe defeated the Lune Road side on the Monday and went to the top of the table. Kruger returned 7-37 and then took 6-25 as Chorley were bowled out for 74 two weeks later. Victories against the two Leyland teams by nine wickets on each occasion in early July put the side challenging for top position.

At this point in the season it was known that Kruger would have to leave for approximately four weeks in flying to Australia to represent South Africa in an Emerging Players tournament that also included the hosts Australia, New Zealand, and Karnataka (India). Availability of quality substitute professionals at this point in mid season was limited and the club made a decision to invest in another flight from South Africa to bring over Quinton Friend, a similar paced bowler to Kruger who had in 2004 been the professional at East Lancs club in the Lancashire League. Friend's presence kept the momentum with the team as he scored 49 in the defeat of Kendal and then took 4-62 and 35 not out and Mark Woodhead 62 in moving to the top of the table against Blackpool on the 22nd July. A heavy defeat at Darwen refocused efforts and against Carnforth at Lodge Quarry the home team after making 235 could only chase the leather after Woodhead was an early loss, as Lomas (100 not out) and Dennison (110 not out) took the side home. This was the first time in the club's history that two players had made a century in the same game.

As the final run-in commenced against St Annes at Woodhill Lane the visitors set the home team 198 to win and with 40 required from the final four overs the game looked destined for a draw until Gareth Pedder with four sixes and one four in a 12- ball 29 enabled Morecambe to reach their victory target in the last over. A poor draw against Leyland Motors followed and the following week was a washout. Kruger was then called back to South Africa to prepare for the domestic season and once again the scramble for substitute professionals commenced. Playing second placed Netherfield on the August bank holiday Saturday a little known Pakistani, Rehman with little first-class experience deputized against Netherfield and took 2-53 as Netherfield batted first and put up a formidable 237-8. In reply the sub pro made 53 as he supported Phil Dennison's 125 not out to secure victory and put one hand on the league championship. On Monday against Lancaster in the traditional derby fixture Indian spinner Sunil Joshi deputized as Morecambe made 263-3 and Lancaster 162-2 from 40 overs before rain curtailed the game leaving Morecambe requiring just two points from the final two games to be certain of outright victory.

The following weekend saw Morecambe crowned league champions as the programme suffered a complete washout. Victory in the final game by 60 runs with Tommy Clough making 83 against Chorley saw League Chairman Norman Poole present the League Trophy to Mark Lomas before the commencement of play. Solid performances with the bat throughout the season from Lomas 662 runs, Thornton 535, Dennison 634, and Woodhead 295 were the basis of many a run chase. With the ball Kruger managed 39 wickets in his brief stay but leading wicket taker was Gareth Pedder with 44 supported by Gates and Lee. This was the first title since 1995 and the fourth in the club's Northern League history. What was clearly different to those previous wins was no outstanding performance in terms of the professional's contribution.

Hilton and Haynes won matches on their own performances whereas this team's success can be attributed to the all- round contribution of the amateur members.

This was a season of 'another first' as the clubs 2nd XI took the second division championship on the last day of season. In the reverse fixture against Chorley Morecambe secured a 15-point victory meaning that Lancaster, batting second at third placed St Annes would only be able to achieve a maximum 12 and therefore allow Morecambe to win the championship be the slimmest margin of one point. This was the second team's sixth championship since its first in 1991. Instrumental in that significant victory against Chorley was Gulam Maje whose score of 76 took his aggregate league tally for the season up to 1,005. No other Division Two player has achieved this and the club can rightly claim another first. This 'double' achievement never being recorded by the club previously and surely must be regarded as the one of the club's finest ever seasons.

After the success of 2006 the club signed South African Werner Coetsee as the club's professional. An accomplished all rounder he scored 877 runs and took 50 wickets as the 1st XI just failed to emulate the previous season's championship win in finishing runners-up this time in one of the closest finishes the league had seen. Vishal Goyal was the leading amateur batsman in scoring 663 runs with a best score of 134 not out, batting superbly against Darwen at Birch Hall. Gates, Pedder and Lee supported the professional with the ball as the side challenged for top spot throughout the season. With the demise of Leyland Motors the League was left with an odd number of clubs which in turn meant two blank fixtures for each club.

Morecambe's 'blank' was the last Saturday of the season and prior to the final weekend they had comprehensively beaten Chorley at Woodhill Lane for 15 points. This left the situation that St Annes must win at Netherfield to secure the title. Netherfield, batting first, amassed 190-6 and when St Annes had lost half their batting for less than 50 it would be fair to say the Morecambe players present at the game thought the title would be theirs. St Annes rallied however and got over the line with two wickets to spare in the last over. The second team did not get quite as close finishing fourth although they did win the second division cup beating Leyland in the final.

In November 2007 at the clubs Annual General Meeting the following officials President Paul Speak, Chairman Ian Hanson, Treasurer Sue Hanson and Secretary Frank Wilkinson all stepped down from office

2008 Cup Winning Team

after amalgamating a huge length of service that the new regime recognised by organising a formal function for the former incumbents with members, family and friends in the clubhouse.

Memories will be fresh for many readers of the team's exploits in 2008 and 2009. New Zealander Bruce Martin was the club professional in 2008 taking 58 wickets and scoring just short of 500 runs in a season ravaged by rain. Graham Lee had a successful season in taking 42 wickets at 16.05 apiece and Vishal Goyal completed his third season scoring a creditable 524 runs. The first team did win the knock-out cup. Playing Preston at the third attempt they had a small victory by just five runs at Woodhill Lane. This was Gareth Pedder's last season at the club as he moved to take up the professional's position at Carnforth and the club looked forward to the 2009 season.

Mark Lomas returned to East Lancs after the first five games of the season and Tommy Clough took over as skipper. Vishal Goyal returned to India mid season after completing his studies at Lancaster University. Charles Boucher, well known in Northern League circles joined for the start of the season and Ikram Ullah, a prolific batsman from Kendal joined the club mid season from Kendal. After original professional Wayne Parnell took the alternative route into the county championship with Kent the club was forced to look elsewhere and hired the popular Mandla Mashimbyi from the Northerns team in

South Africa. Taking 53 wickets and scoring over 400 league runs in another rain-hit season the popular professional showed some awesome hitting in the 20/20 and league cup games. A fifth place finish and Lancashire Cup place resulted as the playing side of the club again moved into a transitional change period.

As this book is in the process of being produced new history is being made in that Mark Woodhead after 20 years has scored his first league century in the first game of the 2010 season at Netherfield.

So that brings me to close of play. I expect that some of the events from my research has rekindled memories for people who either play, officiate, or support the club and for that reason I decided to put into print a history of the club and detail some of the personalities and memories of years gone by. I have no doubt that some of the dialogue will create debate and I fully expect to be challenged on certain opinions and facts within the book so my apologies if any statistics are inconsistent.

Statistics

1. RECORD OF RENNIE NUTTER'S 102 WICKETS IN THE NORTH LANCASHIRE LEAGUE 1937.

2. SCORECARDS OF COLIN HILTON'S 19 WICKETS IN TWO CONSECUTIVE LEAGUE GAMES IN 1969

3. DETAILS OF CURRENT CLUB RECORD HOLDERS

4. RECORD OF ALL MORECAMBE PLAYERS TAKING 8 WICKETS OR SCORING A CENTURY SINCE THE FORMATION OF THE NORTHERN LEAGUE IN 1952.

5. PLAYING RECORD OF CLUBS 1st & 2nd X1 SINCE NORTHERN LEAGUE FORMATION.

6. SCORECARDS OF ALL 1st X1 CUP FINALS.

1. RECORD OF RENNIE NUTTER'S 102 WICKETS IN THE NORTH LANCASHIRE LEAGUE 1937.

Rennie Nutter—Morecambe C.C. Professional 1937-1939

Who took 102 North Lancashire League wickets for Morecambe Cricket Club during the 1937 cricket season.

Details of this achievement are as follows:-

Club	Venue	Overs	Mdnes	Runs	Wkts
Netherfield	Away	12	4	29	4
Dalton	Home	12.4	2	23	9
Ulverston	Away	13	3	32	5
Vickerstown	Home	16	3	41	4
Vickerstown	Away	16	4	28	4
Carnforth	Away	13.1	5	17	7
Carnforth	Home	-	-	-	-
Dalton	Away	21	7	42	3
Millom	Away	17	6	25	4
Ulverston	Home	16.3	4	22	6
Lindal Moor	Home	17	7	27	4
Lindal Moor	Away	21	10	17	5
Kendal	Away	25	6	60	3
Kendal	Away	16.2	3	26	6
Millom	Home	17.4	3	39	7
Netherfield	Home	6.4	1	20	6
Haverigg	Home	14.5	7	19	8
Barrow	Away	18	4	24	3
Barrow	Home	16.1	6	19	8
Haverigg	Away	16	6	44	6
Totals		298	91	554	102

Average	5.43				
5+ Wickets	10				
Econ Rate	1.85				
Strike Rate	17.5				
Home Matches		107.3	33	210	52
Away Matches		190.3	58	344	50

2.SCORECARDS OF COLIN HILTON'S 19 WICKETS IN TWO CONSECUTIVE LEAGUE GAMES IN 1969

NORTHERN LEAGUE
MORECAMBE V LANCASTER

LANCASTER

Batsman	How Out	Bowler	Runs
G.BATES	BOWLED	HILTON	5
S.A.WESTLEY	BOWLED	HILTON	21
M.HALL	BOWLED	HILTON	3
N.ANDREWS	BOWLED	HILTON	1
K.MOORE	BOWLED	HILTON	13
R.B.WESTLEY	BOWLED	HILTON	4
K.HIGGINS	BOWLED	HILTON	0
D.PARKER	NOT OUT		13
T.G.HALL	BOWLED	HILTON	2
R.J.PARKINSON	C.GILES	HILTON	2
D.PEARSON	BOWLED	HILTON	4
		Extras	10
		Total (for 10 wkts)	**78**

Morecambe Bowling :

C.HILTON	14.6	4	34	10
R.JAGGER	6	1	18	0
A.JAGGER	8	2	16	0

MORECAMBE

Batsman	How Out	Bowler	Runs
G.ROBINSON	C.PEARSON	PARKER	10
R.MASHITER	C.T.G.HALL	PARKER	1
C.CLOUGH	C.T.G.HALL	PARKER	23
R.SANDHAM	LBW	PARKER	24
A.EVANS	NOT OUT		7
F.WILKINSON	C.S.WESTLEY	PEARSON	3
D.HASTINGS	NOT OUT		0
		Extras	14
		Total (for 5 wkts)	**82**

Lancaster Bowling :

D.PEARSON	7.6	1	27	1
D.PARKER	10	1	31	4
N.ANDREWS	3	0	10	0

NORTHERN LEAGUE
MORECAMBE V KENDAL
MORECAMBE

Batsman	How Out	Bowler	Runs
G.ROBINSON	C.ALLEN	EVANS	24
R.MASHITER	C.GUNNING	ALLEN	32
I.GRAY	LBW	EMERSON	0
R.SANDHAM	BOWLED	EMERSON	1
A.EVANS	RUN OUT		9
H.GILES	C.HARRISON	PARSONS	12
F.WILKINSON	BOWLED	EMERSON	11
A.JAGGER	BOWLED	PARSONS	6
C.HILTON	C.PARSONS	EVANS	22
H.CLARKSON	BOWLED	EMERSON	0
R.JAGGER	NOT OUT		1
		Extras	6
		Total (for 10 wkts)	**124**

Kendal Bowling :

N.EMERSON	13	3	36	4
B.PARSONS	12	5	27	1
B.EVANS	6	1	25	2
M.ALLEN	6.4	1	30	2

KENDAL

Batsman	How Out	Bowler	Runs
B.HARRISON	LBW	HILTON	0
G.CATHEY	BOWLED	HILTON	4
T.GUNNING	C.MASHITER	HILTON	14
I.HOWSON	BOWLED	HILTON	2
P.R.SMITH	BOWLED	HILTON	2
B.PARSONS	C.CLARKSON	HILTON	1
B.EVANS	C.HILTON	JAGGER	6
N.EMERSON	BOWLED	HILTON	19
M.ALLEN	C.CLARKSON	HILTON	38
P.EVANS	BOWLED	HILTON	11
M.ARCHER	NOT OUT		1
		extras	11
		Total (for 10 wkts)	**109**

Morecambe Bowling :

C.HILTON	19.6	9	42	9
A.JAGGER	6	2	22	0
R.JAGGER	10	2	21	1
H.CLARKSON	3	0	13	0

3. DETAILS OF CURRENT CLUB RECORD HOLDERS

FARUK PATEL

Who set a new Northern League amateur bowling record for Morecambe Cricket Club 2nd XI during the 2004 cricket season.

Details of this achievement are as follows:-

Club	Venue	Overs	Mdnes	Runs	Wkts
Barrow	Home	11	0	47	2
Barrow	Away	22	5	71	6
Blackpool	Home	18	4	62	5
Blackpool	Away	13	2	38	4
Chorley	Home	17	3	62	2
Chorley	Away	11	5	17	2
Darwen	Home	12	1	43	1
Darwen	Away	13	5	12	6
Fleetwood	Home	17	6	32	5
Fleetwood	Away	11	3	43	4
Kendal	Home	24	5	68	3
Kendal	Away	16	2	32	7
Lancaster	Home	20	7	37	5
Lancaster	Away	13.4	6	26	5
Leyland	Home	9.3	1	27	2
Leyland	Away	12	4	17	4
Leyland Motors	Home	12	3	30	5
Leyland Motors	Away	18	9	32	5
Netherfield	Home	12	0	60	1
Netherfield	Away	0	0	0	0
Preston	Home	11	2	29	1
Preston	Away	0	0	0	0
St Annes	Home	17	8	36	5
St Annes	Away	18	2	64	1
Totals		328.1	83	885	81
Average		10.93			
5+ Wickets		10			
Econ Rate		2.70			
Strike Rate		24.31			
Home Matches		180.3	40	533	37
Away Matches		147.4	43	252	44

GULAM MAJE

Who set a new Northern League amateur batting record for Morecambe Cricket Club 2nd XI during the 2006 cricket season.

He became the first to reach 1000 runs in Division 2 of the League

Details of this achievement are as follows:-

Club	Venue	Innings	Not Out	Runs
Barrow	Home	1		0
Barrow	Away	1		33
Blackpool	Home	1		40
Blackpool	Away	1		54
Carnforth	Home	1		62
Carnforth	Away			
Chorley	Home	1		76
Chorley	Away	1		43
Darwen	Home	1		13
Darwen	Away	1		66
Fleetwood	Home	1		3
Fleetwood	Away			
Kendal	Home	1		44
Kendal	Away	1		3
Lancaster	Home	1		9
Lancaster	Away	1		8
Leyland	Home	1		48
Leyland	Away	1		61
Leyland Motors	Home	1		30
Leyland Motors	Away	1	1	60
Netherfield	Home	1		5
Netherfield	Away	1		94
Preston	Home			
Preston	Away	1		87
St Annes	Home	1		22
St Annes	Away	1		54
Totals		23	1	1005
Average		45.68		
X 50		10		
X 100				
Home Matches		12		352
Away Matches		11	1	653

PHILIP THORNTON

Who set a new Northern League amateur batting record for Morecambe Cricket Club 1st XI during the 2001 cricket season.

Details of this achievement are as follows:-

Club	Venue	Innings	Not Out	Runs
Blackpool	Home	1		0
Blackpool	Away	1		27
Chorley	Home	1	1	12
Chorley	Away	1		69
Darwen	Home	1		113
Darwen	Away	1		80
Fleetwood	Home	1		70
Fleetwood	Away	1	1	61
Kendal	Home	1		6
Kendal	Away	1		20
Lancaster	Home	1		10
Lancaster	Away			
Leyland	Home	1	1	121
Leyland	Away	1		22
Leyland Motors	Home	1		29
Leyland Motors	Away	1		38
Netherfield	Home	1		35
Netherfield	Away	1		67
Preston	Home	1		37
Preston	Away	1		28
St Annes	Home	1		26
St Annes	Away	1		0
Totals		21	3	871
Average		48.39		
X 50		5		
X 100		2		
Home Matches		11	2	459
Away Matches		10	1	412

PETER STEPHENS

Who set a new Northern League amateur bowling record for Morecambe Cricket Club 1st XI during the 2002 cricket season.

Details of this achievement are as follows:-

Club	Venue	Overs	Mdnes	Runs	Wkts
Blackpool	Home	25	8	59	4
Blackpool	Away	20	9	27	5
Chorley	Home	23	6	44	4
Chorley	Away	23	7	55	6
Darwen	Home	0	0	0	0
Darwen	Away	28	9	55	6
Fleetwood	Home	14	4	33	4
Fleetwood	Away	8	2	44	0
Kendal	Home	11	1	38	1
Kendal	Away	0	0	0	0
Lancaster	Home	24.2	9	32	7
Lancaster	Away	25	3	67	5
Leyland	Home	28	6	72	2
Leyland	Away	14	3	49	2
Leyland Motors	Home	13	4	29	4
Leyland Motors	Away	23	7	45	6
Netherfield	Home	19	7	39	4
Netherfield	Away	16.1	5	30	7
Preston	Home	20	7	37	4
Preston	Away	29	6	59	1
St Annes	Home	29	5	85	2
St Annes	Away	15	2	62	1
Totals		407.3	110	961	75
Average		12.81			
5+ Wickets		7			
Econ Rate		2.36			
Strike Rate		32.58			
Home Matches		206.2	57	468	36
Away Matches		201.1	53	493	39

COLIN HILTON

Who set a new Northern League professional bowling record for Morecambe Cricket Club 1st XI during the 1968 cricket season.

Details of this achievement are as follows:-

Club	Venue	Overs	Mdnes	Runs	Wkts
Blackpool	Home	10	2	50	6
Blackpool	Away	14	1	69	4
Chorley	Home	15.6	2	38	4
Chorley	Away	12	4	41	8
Darwen	Home	7.6	3	21	4
Darwen	Away	19.7	3	64	6
Fleetwood	Home	8	2	28	6
Fleetwood	Away	14.1	9	9	8
Kendal	Home	6.5	0	12	7
Kendal	Away	21.2	3	55	4
Lancaster	Home	22.4	6	56	6
Lancaster	Away	22	2	61	3
Leyland	Home	16	1	13	8
Leyland	Away	9.7	1	65	3
Leyland Motors	Home	11	5	40	4
Leyland Motors	Away	17.7	2	47	4
Netherfield	Home	13	4	32	7
Netherfield	Away	0	0	0	0
Preston	Home	18.1	2	45	3
Preston	Away	19.7	7	43	8
St Annes	Home	16.4	4	33	5
St Annes	Away	16.2	0	56	5
Totals		312.3	63	878	113
Average		7.7			
5+ Wickets		12			
Econ Rate		2.81			
Strike Rate		22.12			
Home Matches		151.3	38	349	62
Away Matches		161	25	529	51

STEVEN POPE

Who set a new Northern League professional batting record for Morecambe Cricket Club 1st XI during the 1996 cricket season.

Details of this achievement are as follows:-

Club	Venue	Innings	Not Out	Runs
Blackpool	Home			
Blackpool	Away	1		99
Chorley	Home			
Chorley	Away	1		84
Darwen	Home	1		36
Darwen	Away	1		50
Fleetwood	Home	1		4
Fleetwood	Away	1		45
Kendal	Home	1	1	86
Kendal	Away	1	1	78
Lancaster	Home	1		120
Lancaster	Away	1		55
Leyland	Home	1	1	63
Leyland	Away	1		44
Leyland Motors	Home	1		29
Leyland Motors	Away	1		0
Netherfield	Home	1	1	96
Netherfield	Away	1		17
Preston	Home	1		3
Preston	Away	1	1	77
St Annes	Home	1	0	27
St Annes	Away	1	1	74
Totals		20	6	1117
Average		79.79		
X 50		10		
X 100		1		
Home Matches		9	3	494
Away Matches		11	3	623

4. RECORD OF ALL MORECAMBE PLAYERS TAKING 8 WICKETS OR SCORING A CENTURY SINCE THE FORMATION OF THE NORTHERN LEAGUE IN 1952.

Morecambe CC
Centuries in Northern League 1952-2009, First XI

Season	Player	Scores
1952	JE Haigh	101
1953	JF Parker	134*, 107
1961	D Garner	123
1962	G Houlton	112*
1965	G Houlton	106
1968	R Wrightson	113
1970	D Bailey	109
1975	A Robinson	113*
1985	R Shastri	136*, 103
1986	G Fisher	149*, 105*, 102*, 101
1987	G Fisher	129*
1989	R Haynes	138, 126*
	G Fisher	102*
1990	C Knight	154
1991	R Haynes	103*, 103, 102*
	G Fisher	111
1992	R Haynes	113, 104*
1994	G Fisher	111*
	R Haynes	100*
1995	G Fisher	110*
1996	S Pope	120
1997	S Pope	113*
1998	S Pope	132, 104*, 100
1999	A Prince	106
2000	A Prince	114
2001	P Thornton	121*, 113
	A Muzumdar	106, 100*
2002	R Powar	111*
	R Morris	134
2003	P Dennison	104
2004	C Langeveldt	156
2005	M Orchard	111, 117
2006	P Dennison	110*, 125*
	M Lomas	100*
2007	V Goyal	134*
	W Coetsee	110*
	R Ali	108*
2009	C Boucher	119

Morecambe CC
Centuries in Northern League 1952-2009
Second XI

Season Player Scores

1955	HB Moseley	130
1960	H Giles	143
1962	J Normanton	100*
1964	J Normanton	116*
1965	F Normanton	103*
1968	R Sandham	100*
1972	F Normanton	101*
1976	F Wilkinson	137*
1981	K Moore	102*
1989	P Thornton	140
1991	M Mace	105*
	P Thornton	101*
1993	A Speak	109*

	P Moffat	107
1995	K Demain	102
1997	S Lord	105*
1998	K Demain	103
1999	I Izzat	109*, 108*
2001	M Fisher	113
	I Izzat	102*
2004	G Pedder	102
2006	B Akrigg	140*
2007	G Maje	102, 114, 104
	B Akrigg	101*
2008	B Akrigg	104
2009	G Maje	100

Morecambe CC
Eight wickets in an innings in Northern League 1952-2009
First XI

Season Player Analysis

1956	RS Miller	9-27
1960	R Jagger	8-45
1966	EA Kelly	8-38
1968	C Hilton	8-9, 8-13, 8-41, 8-43
1969	C Hilton	10-34, 9-42, 8-38
1970	R Jagger	8-41
1973	C Hilton	8-28
1977	C Gradwell	8-23
1988	G Sharma	8-16
1992	R Haynes	8-30
1993	R Haynes	8-45
	F Patel	9-42
1995	R Haynes	8-53, 8-68
2004	C Langeveldt	8-63, 8-38, 8-48
2007	J Gates	8-59

Morecambe CC
Eight wickets in an innings in Northern League 1952-2009

Second XI

Season Player Analysis

1957	J Mulroy	8-17
1959	J Simpson	8-32
1960	R Worthington	8-17
1966	T Holgate	9-39
1967	R Jagger	9-49
1981	N Marsdin	8-50
1982	M Armistead	8-40
	N Marsdin	8-56
1987	M Armistead	9-33
1990	M Armistead	9-62
1991	J Butler	8-51
1992	M Armistead	8-49
1996	G Kershaw	8-42
2002	J Gates	8-26
2003	G Lee	8-15, 8-51
2007	P Stephens	8-25
	W Quinn	8-34

5. PLAYING RECORD OF CLUBS 1st & 2nd X1 SINCE NORTHERN LEAGUE FORMATION.

MORECAMBE FIRST XI NORTHERN LEAGUE RECORD

Season	Played	Won	Drawn	Lost	Pos
1952	20	2	12	6	8
1953	22	6	11	5	6
1954	22	6	10	6	6
1955	22	5	10	7	9
1956	22	9	8	5	5
1957	22	5	10	7	9
1958	22	5	9	8	12
1959	22	5	8	9	9
1960	22	5	11	6	8
1961	22	2	9	11	11
1962	22	2	8	12	11
1963	22	1	16	5	12
1964	22	4	8	10	11
1965	22	2	12	8	10
1966	22	2	10	10	11
1967	22	3	9	10	11
1968	22	13	3	6	1
1969	22	10	5	7	4
1970	22	5	5	12	9
1971	22	4	5	13	12
1972	22	1	7	14	12
1973	22	4	4	14	11
1974	22	1	7	14	12
1975	22	3	4	15	12
1976	22	4	7	11	10
1977	22	2	11	9	11
1978	22	5	8	9	9
1979	22	3	10	9	9
1980	22	5	10	7	9
1981	22	2	10	10	12
1982	22	5	11	6	7
1983	22	4	16	2	4
1984	22	7	7	8	7
1985	22	5	15	2	3
1986	22	3	11	8	9
1987	22	7	10	5	5
1988	22	7	9	6	6
1989	22	4	8	10	9
1990	22	10	4	8	4
1991	22	5	10	7	8
1992	22	7	13	2	1
1993	22	9	8	5	5
1994	22	6	11	5	6
1995	22	15	4	3	1
1996	22	9	10	3	3
1997	22	4	15	3	6
1998	22	6	12	4	9
1999	22	7	9	6	5
2000	22	8	10	4	4
2001	22	5	15	2	7
2002	22	15	4	3	2
2003	22	10	5	7	5
2004	24	12	6	6	4
2005	24	9	10	5	6
2006	26	16	7	3	1
2007	24	12	8	4	2
2008	24	10	11	3	4
2009	24	7	12	5	5
TOTAL	**1288**	**350**	**528**	**410**	

MORECAMBE SECOND XI NORTHERN LEAGUE RECORD

Season	Played	Won	Drawn	Lost	Pos
1952	20	5	9	6	7
1953	22	6	10	6	7
1954	22	4	6	12	11
1955	22	10	2	10	6
1956	22	5	4	13	10
1957	22	4	4	14	12
1958	22	5	3	14	12
1959	22	4	3	15	11
1960	22	9	3	10	4
1961	22	3	7	12	12
1962	22	4	4	14	11
1963	22	3	5	14	11
1964	22	3	9	10	11
1965	22	8	2	12	8
1966	22	6	6	10	10
1967	22	5	8	9	10
1968	22	4	4	14	10
1969	22	5	3	14	11
1970	22	6	8	8	10

Season	Played	Won	Drawn	Lost	Pos
1971	22	3	7	12	11
1972	22	5	8	9	9
1973	22	0	7	15	12
1974	22	1	5	16	12
1975	22	4	2	16	12
1976	22	4	11	7	9
1977	22	10	5	7	4
1978	22	4	7	11	11
1979	22	4	12	6	9
1980	22	6	12	4	6
1981	22	4	9	9	9
1982	22	9	7	6	5
1983	22	7	12	3	2
1984	22	5	8	9	7
1985	22	4	15	3	7
1986	22	5	10	7	7
1987	22	7	10	5	6
1988	22	10	9	3	2
1989	22	11	7	4	3
1990	22	12	5	5	3
1991	22	13	7	2	1

Season	Played	Won	Drawn	Lost	Pos
1992	22	5	15	2	4
1993	22	9	8	5	3
1994	22	12	9	1	1
1995	22	7	9	6	4
1996	22	4	11	7	8
1997	22	6	10	6	5
1998	22	12	7	3	2
1999	22	16	5	1	1
2000	22	9	10	3	3
2001	22	10	8	4	4
2002	22	13	7	2	1
2003	22	7	10	5	5
2004	24	16	7	1	1
2005	24	12	8	4	3
2006	26	13	10	3	1
2007	24	10	8	6	4
2008	24	6	13	5	6
2009	24	8	11	5	7
TOTAL	**1288**	**402**	**441**	**445**	

6. SCORECARDS OF ALL 1st X1 CUP FINALS.

HIGSON CUP FINAL 1927

FURNESS v MORECAMBE

FURNESS

Batsman	How Out	Bowler	Runs
W.H.DODD	BOWLED	NOBLE	8
W.B.COLLINGE	C.NOBLE	THOMPSON	1
W.DOIDGE	BOWLED	HUSTLER	43
A.BOOTH	LBW THOMPSON		2
F.MERCER	BOWLED	NOBLE	0
C.H.DOIDGE	C.SIMPSON	THOMPSON	4
W.G.COLLINGE snr	C.FOLEY	SIMPSON	29
J.MELVILLE	C.CROWTHER	SIMPSON	5
A.PATTERSON	NOT OUT		7
A.I.FULLER	C.SIMPSON	HUSTLER	11
H.OGDEN	RUN OUT		0
		Extras	11
		Total (for 10 wkts)	121

Morecambe Bowling :

J.THOMPSON	22	7	54	3
L.NOBLE	17	4	35	2
T.HUSTLER	6	1	12	2
W.SIMPSON	6	4	9	2

MORECAMBE

Batsman	How Out	Bowler	Runs
W.H.WILKINSON	C AND B	COLLINGE	11
J.S.CROWTHER	C.MERCER	COLLINGE	8
L.NOBLE	C.OGDEN	MELVILLE	19
H.FOLEY	C.MELVVILLE	COLLINGE	25
T.HUSTLER	C.DOIDGE	MELVILLE	7
J.THORNTON	BOWLED	MELVILLE	2
J.THOMPSON	BOWLED	MELVILLE	0
T.HUNT	LBW	OGDEN	6
F.BLAND	BOWLED	MELVILLE	0
W.SIMPSON	BOWLED	MELVILLE	5
J.R.RICHARDSON	NOT OUT		5
		Extras	18
		Total (for 10 wkts)	106

Furness Bowling :

W.G.COLLINGE	20	6	39	3
H.OGDEN	8.2	2	21	1
J.MELVILLE	13	2	23	6

SLATER CUP FINAL 1965

MORECAMBE V LEYLAND MOTORS

MORECAMBE

Batsman	How Out	Bowler	Runs
G.HOULTON	ST.AINSCOUGH	SOUTHWORTH	67
F.WILKINSON	C AND B	MAHAWATTE	58
C.CLOUGH	C.RIMMER	SOUTHWORTH	4
K.BEAL	BOWLED	ASHCROFT	13
H.GILES	RUN OUT		31
G.LUNN	NOT OUT		7
R.MASHITER	BOWLED	ASHCROFT	2
T.BENTLEY	BOWLED	ASHCROFT	2
R.JAGGER	BOWLED	BOLTON	5
A.JAGGER	NOT OUT		5
I.HANSON			
		Extras	5
		Total (for 8 wkts)	199

Leyland Motors Bowling :

T.ASHCROFT	7	0	27	3
P.MAHAWATTE	5	0	37	1
R.BOLTON	7	0	45	1
G.MORRIS	1	0	25	0
R.SOUTHWORTH	7	0	38	2
D.BARNES	3	0	23	0

LEYLAND MOTORS

Batsman	How Out	Bowler	Runs
P.MAHAWATTE	C WILKINSON	R.JAGGER	43
D.RIMMER	C.BEAL	A.JAGGER	10
D.LEADBETTER	BOWLED	HOULTON	32
D.PORTER	C.HANSON	HOULTON	0
G.MORRIS	BOWLED	R.JAGGER	3
T.ASHCROFT	BOWLED	CLOUGH	4
M.HOWARD	BOWLED	CLOUGH	5
D.BARNES	BOWLED	R.JAGGER	2
R.SOUTHWORTH	NOT OUT		8
E.AINSCOUGH	LBW	BEAL	9
R.BOLTON	C.GILES	BEAL	0
		Extras	3
		Total (for 10 wkts)	119

Morecambe Bowling :

G.HOULTON	7	0	33	2
R.JAGGER	7	1	18	3
A.JAGGER	7	0	34	1
K.BEAL	7	0	1	2
C.CLOUGH	7	0	30	2

SLATER CUP FINAL 1968

MORECAMBE V LEYLAND

LEYLAND

Batsman	How Out	Bowler	Runs
A.ALKER	BOWLED	HILTON	2
R.LEE	BOWLED	HILTON	4
C.BROWN	BOWLED	A.JAGGER	10
D.WAREING	LBW	HILTON	4
D.HALLIWELL	C.WRIGHTSON	A.JAGGER	0
P.WAREING	RUN OUT		4
T.ASHCROFT	C.WRIGHTSON	CLOUGH	24
D.BROWN	BOWLED	CLOUGH	2
J.W.McKITTRICK	NOT OUT		11
J.HAYNES	BOWLED	CLOUGH	0
A.WATSON	BOWLED	CLOUGH	1
		Extras	12
		Total (for 10 wkts)	74

Morecambe Bowling :

C.HILTON	7	2	9	3
A.JAGGER	7	2	15	2
C.CLOUGH	6.6	0	26	4
R.JAGGER	6	0	12	0

MORECAMBE

Batsman	How Out	Bowler	Runs
G.ROBINSON	C.LEE	McKITTRICK	12
D.HASTINGS	BOWLED	ASHCROFT	0
R.WRIGHTSON	LBW	HALLIWELL	17
F.WILKINSON	BOWLED	HALLIWELL	0
C.HILTON	BOWLED	HALLIWELL	14
C.CLOUGH	LBW	HALLIWELL	3
H.GILES	NOT OUT		14
W.BLAND	NOT OUT		17
		Extras	0
		Total (for 6 wkts)	77

Leyland Bowling :

T.ASHCROFT	7	1	23	1
J.HAYNES	1	0	10	0
J.W.McKITTRICK	7	1	18	1
A.WATSON	1	0	10	0
D.HALLIWELL	7	2	16	4

MATTHEW BROWN TROPHY CUP FINAL 1987

LEYLAND v MORECAMBE

MORECAMBE

Batsman	How Out	Bowler	Runs
M.PICKLES	C. K.SNELLGROVE	WESTWOOD	13
G.FISHER	C.D.SNELLGROVE	GILMORE	5
A.SPEAK	C.SERGEANT	WESTWOOD	2
C.SHARMA	C.HAYES	K.SNELLGROVE	23
P.THORNTON	C.WESTWOOD	TENNANT	12
K.DEMAIN	LBW	K.SNELLGROVE	8
K.RILEY	BOWLED	D.SNELLGROVE	0
M.BREZINKA	BOWLED	WESTWOOD	18
J.BUTLER	BOWLED	TENNANT	0
I.LEDWARD	C.PALLETT	K.SNELLGROVE	0
N.MARSDIN	NOT OUT		1
		Extras	8
		Total (for 10 wkts)	90

Leyland Bowling :

E.WESTWOOD	6.6	2	16	3
K.SNELLGROVE	7	2	17	3
G.GILMORE	6	1	19	1
D.SNELLGROVE	2	0	10	1
B.TENNANT	7	1	20	2

LEYLAND

Batsman	How Out	Bowler	Runs
A.HESKETH	NOT OUT		51
K.SNELLGROVE	BOWLED	BUTLER	10
D.SNELLGROVE	RUN OUT		3
T.HAYES	C.RILEY	MARSDIN	4
J.FAZACKERLEY	NOT OUT		13
		Extras	10
		Total (for 3 wkts)	91

Morecambe Bowling :

C.SHARMA	7	0	21	0
I.LEDWARD	4.4	0	20	0
J.BUTLER	6	0	26	1
M.BREZINKA	0.4	0	8	0
N.MARSDIN	1.4	0	9	1

SLALOM LAGER CUP FINAL 1990

LEYLAND MOTORS v MORECAMBE

MORECAMBE

Batsman	How Out	Bowler	Runs
C.KNIGHT	C.MAKINSON	PRINCE	14
G.FISHER	BOWLED	MAKINSON	64
S.SMITH	C.WILLIAMS	LAMBERT	36
C.ATKINS	C.PATEL	TOWNSON	5
P.THORNTON	NOT OUT		35
R.PATEL	C.FAZACKERLEY	MAKINSON	2
M.LAMB	NOT OUT		1
K.RILEY			
G.MAJE			
M.ARMISTEAD			
I.LEDWARD			
		Extras	25
		Total (for 5 wkts)	182

Leyland Motors Bowling :

D.MAKINSON	8	2	34	2
P.DEAKIN	8	0	47	0
S.PRINCE	8	0	30	1
M.TOWNSON	8	0	17	1
P.LAMBERT	8	1	35	1

LEYLAND MTRS

Batsman	How Out	Bowler	Runs
D.PATEL	C.THORNTON	ARMISTEAD	15
J.FAZACKERLEY	C.THORNTON	ARMISTEAD	36
M.PASS	BOWLED	MAJE	2
D.MAKINSON	BOWLED	ARMISTEAD	5
P.PATEL	C.RILEY	ATKINS	10
S.HENDERSON	C.KNIGHT	ATKINS	9
M.TOWNSON	RUN OUT		18
P.DEAKIN	RUN OUT		4
C.WILLIAMS	BOWLED	PATEL	7
P.LAMBERT	BOWLED	PATEL	1
S.PRINCE	NOT OUT		0
		Extras	21
		Total (for 10 wkts)	128

Morecambe Bowling :

R.PATEL	6.6	0	15	2
G.MAJE	8	4	10	1
I.LEDWARD	8	1	38	0
C.ATKINS	7	3	15	2
M.ARMISTEAD	8	0	31	3

MATTHEW BROWN CUP FINAL 1990

MORECAMBE V KENDAL

MORECAMBE

Batsman	How Out	Bowler	Runs
C.KNIGHT	C AND B	HUNTE	71
G.FISHER	LBW	POTTS	53
P.THORNTON	BOWLED	POTTS	21
S.SMITH	BOWLED	POTTS	8
C.ATKINS	NOT OUT		35
R.PATEL	NOT OUT		2
M.LAMB			
K.RILEY			
G.MAJE			
M.ARMISTEAD			
I.LEDWARD			
		Extras	26
		Total (for 4 wkts)	183

Kendal Bowling :

K.BARNES	6	1	25	0
A.POTTS	6	0	38	3
A.WILSON	6	0	23	0
M.WILLIAMS	6	0	44	0
T.HUNTE	6	0	29	1

KENDAL

Batsman	How Out	Bowler	Runs
P.STEWART	BOWLED	PATEL	3
S.STUART	C.THORNTON	PATEL	1
T.HUNTE	C.KNIGHT	THORNTON	70
A.THOMPSON	C.KNIGHT	ATKINS	7
M.WILLIAMS	BOWLED	MAJE	82
P.FEARNYOUGH	BOWLED	THORNTON	0
S.DAVIDSON	NOT OUT		5
M.WOOD	NOT OUT		0
A.WILSON			
A.POTTS			
K.BARNES			
		Extras	16
		Total (for 6 wkts)	184

Bowling :

R.PATEL	6	3	32	3
G.MAJE	5	0	31	1
I.LEDWARD	6	0	21	0
P.THORNTON	5.7	0	48	2
C.ATKINS	6	0	38	1

THEAKSTON CUP FINAL 1993

MORECAMBE V LEYLAND

LEYLAND

Batsman	How Out	Bowler	Runs
P.SIMMONITE	LBW	HAYNES	5
G.GREENIDGE	C.DERHAM	THORNTON	1
P.BERRY	C.WELBOURNE	DERHAM	39
G.WELLS	ST.RILEY	MAJE	53
D.GREEN	LBW	PATEL	5
T.BARRY	C.WELBOURNE	MAJE	30
B.TENNANT	RUN OUT		17
S.PALLETT	NOT OUT		0
J.WADDINGTON			
R.CUTHBERTSON			
J.FARRAR			
		Extras	11
		Total (for 7 wkts)	161

Morecambe Bowling :

R.HAYNES	6	0	26	1
D.DERHAM	6	0	31	1
P.THORNTON	6	1	22	1
F.PATEL	6	0	30	1
G.MAJE	6	0	43	2

MORECAMBE

Batsman	How Out	Bowler	Runs
G.FISHER	C.WADDINGTON	GREENIDGE	30
M.WOODHEAD	C.BARRY	PALLETT	14
D.WELBOURNE	RUN OUT		5
R.HAYNES	C.BERRY	TENNANT	45
M.LAMB	BOWLED	BARRY	24
P.THORNTON	C.PALLETT	BARRY	13
D.DERHAM	RUN OUT		2
G.MAJE	RUN OUT		4
F.PATEL C.FARRAR	BARRY		2
K.DEMAIN	NOT OUT		1
K.RILEY RUN OUT			0
		Extras	19
		Total (for 10 wkts)	159

Leyland Bowling :

B.TENNANT	6	0	41	1
T.BARRY	6	0	22	3
R.CUTHBERTSON	6	3	8	0
S.PALLETT	6	1	44	1
G.GREENIDGE	6	0	22	3

VAUX BITTER CUP FINAL 1994

DARWEN V MORECAMBE

DARWEN

Batsman	How Out	Bowler	Runs
S.PAINTER	BOWLED	MAJE	17
G.AINSLIE	C.RILEY	DERHAM	32
G.CORDINGLEY	C.MAJE	STEPHENS	30
G.PARKINSON	LBW	PATEL	41
D.BONNER	C.MOFFATT	PATEL	5
M.FRIEND	RUN OUT		13
J.HACKING	NOT OUT		7
I.CRITCHLEY	NOT OUT		1
		Extras	13
		Total (for 6 wkts)	158

Morecambe Bowling :

F.PATEL	8	0	48	2
D.DERHAM	8	0	27	1
P.STEPHENS	8	0	20	1
P.THORNTON	8	0	34	0
G.MAJE	8	0	26	1

MORECAMBE

Batsman	How Out	Bowler	Runs
G.FISHER	BOWLED	CORDINGLEY	11
M.WOODHEAD	C.PAINTER	CORDINGLEY	0
P.MOFFATT	C.PARKINSON	LAWRENSON	18
S.LORD	C.CRITCHLEY	CORDINGLEY	5
P.THORNTON	C.CORDINGLEY	CRITCHLEY	18
D.DERHAM	C.FRIEND	CRITCHLEY	8
G.MAJE	RUN OUT		19
D.WELBOURNE	BOWLED	LAWRENSON	4
F.PATEL	C.PAINTER	JACKSON	5
K.RILEY	C.LAWRENSON	BONNER	3
P.STEPHENS	NOT OUT		1
		Extras	10
		Total (for 10 wkts)	102

Darwen Bowling :

G.CORDINGLEY	8	0	18	3
I.CRITCHLEY	8	0	28	2
D.BONNER	7.4	1	15	1
G.JACKSON	5	0	10	1
G.LAWRENSON	8	0	24	2

VAUX SAMSON CUP FINAL 1997

MORECAMBE V NETHERFIELD

MORECAMBE

Batsman	How Out	Bowler	Runs
G.FISHER	LBW	CROOKES	19
M.WOODHEAD	C.DALZELL	LITTLE	12
S.POPE C.WHITE	WHEATMAN		92
P.MOFFATT	BOWLED	HADWIN	10
D.WEBOURNE	BOWLED	WHEATMAN	9
P.THORNTON	C.WHITE	CROOKES	21
N.JORDAN	NOT OUT		7
J.ECCLES	NOT OUT		0
F.PATEL			
D.GUDGEON			
P.STEPHENS			
		Extras	9
	Total (for 6 wkts)		179

Netherfield Bowling :

D.WHEATMAN	6	1	27	2
D.CROOKES	6	1	51	2
S.LITTLE	6	1	19	1
M.HADWIN	6	0	35	1
S.CLEMENT	6	1	51	2

NETHERFIELD

Batsman	How Out	Bowler	Runs
G.CLARKE	C.GUDGEON	PATEL	0
G.WHITE	RUN OUT		63
D.CROOKES	LBW	JORDAN	16
S.LITTLE	C.STEPHENS	ECCLES	44
S.DALZELL	LBW	PATEL	1
T.PRIME	RUN OUT		8
D.OTWAY	NOT OUT		31
D.WHEATMAN	NOT OUT		5
		Extras	12
	Total (for 6 wkts)		180

Bowling :

F.PATEL	6	0	49	2
S.POPE	3	0	25	0
P.STEPHENS	6	0	14	0
J.ECCLES	6	0	37	1
N.JORDAN	5.5	0	34	1
P.MOFFATT	3	0	15	0

VAUX BITTER CUP FINAL 1997

ST ANNES v MORECAMBE

MORECAMBE

Batsman	How Out	Bowler	Runs
G.FISHER	BOWLED	DAVIES	40
M.WOODHEAD	RUN OUT		72
S.POPE	NOT OUT		59
P.MOFFATT	C.DAVIES	R.BRADLEY	30
P.THORNTON	NOT OUT		16
		Extras	34
	Total (for 3 wkts)		251

St Annes Bowling :

E.BAPTISTE	8	1	34 0
J.DAVIES	6	1	37 1
B.TENNANT	8	1	36 0
R.BRADLEY	2	0	25 1
A.DARLINGTON	8	0	52 0
S.BICKERDIKE	1	0	6 0
I.CRITCHLEY	7	0	47 0

ST ANNES

Batsman	How Out	Bowler	Runs
A.DARLINGTON	C.GUDGEON	PATEL	14
E.BAPTISTE	BOWLED	PATEL	4
C.HARRISON	C.JORDAN	STEPHENS	18
R.BRADLEY	BOWLED	PATEL	1
N.BRADLEY	C.FISHER	STEPHENS	69
S.TWIST	RUN OUT		12
S.BICKERDIKE	ST GUDGEON	POPE	19
I.CRITCHLEY	BOWLED	POPE	8
B.TENNANT	ST GUDGEON	POPE	6
J.DAVIES	C.GUDGEON	STEPHENS	1
S.WHALLEY	NOT OUT		0
		Extras	22
	Total (for 10 wkts)		174

Morecambe Bowling :

F.PATEL	8	0	33	3
J.ECCLES	8	1	42	0
P.STEPHENS	6.1	1	21	3
S.POPE	5	0	22	3
N.JORDAN	6	0	38	0

THEAKSTON CUP FINAL 1999

MORECAMBE V CHORLEY

CHORLEY

Batsman	How Out	Bowler	Runs
J.FAZACKERLEY	RUN OUT		3
R.CAKE	C AND B	ECCLES	28
R.HORRIDGE	BOWLED	CLOUGH	1
N.HEATON	RUN OUT		78
N.SENIOR	BOWLED	ECCLES	13
D.CATTERALL	NOT OUT		25
J.MARQUET	NOT OUT		9
R.PURNELL			
J.GREAVES			
K.ECCLESHARE			
I.PATEL			
		Extras	14
	Total (for 5 wkts)		171

Morecambe Bowling :

P.STEPHENS	8	1	27	0
J.ECCLES	8	0	21	2
T.CLOUGH	4	0	30	1
A.PRINCE	5	0	30	0
G.MAJE	8	0	16	0
G.PEDDER	7	0	38	0

MORECAMBE

Batsman	How Out	Bowler	Runs
M.WOODHEAD	C.HORRIDGE	MARQUET	14
A.PRINCE	RUN OUT		76
G.FISHER	C.HORRIDGE	PURNELL	2
P.THORNTON	ST SENIOR	ECCLESHARE	24
T.CLOUGH	LBW	GREAVES	2
J.ECCLES	C.SENIOR	CATTERALL	24
G.MAJE	NOT OUT		15
A.MASHITER	NOT OUT		12
D. GUDGEON			
P.STEPHENS			
G.PEDDER			
		Extras	6
	Total (for 6 wkts)		175

Chorley Bowling :

I.PATEL	5	1	24	0
K.ECCLESHARE	8	0	29	1
R.PURNELL	8	0	27	1
J.GREAVES	4	1	35	1
J.MARQUET	8	1	35	1
D.CATTERALL	4.2	0	20	1

THWAITES SMOOTH CUP FINAL 2003

MORECAMBE V NETHERFIELD
NETHERFIELD

Batsman	How Out	Bowler	Runs
C.WALMSLEY	C.MASHITER	STEPHENS	9
G.WHITE	C AND B	BIRD	30
G.CLARKE	C.DENNISON	CLOUGH	16
P.STRYDOM	LBW	BIRD	8
R.GIRDHARI	BOWLED	BIRD	7
C.PARRY	BOWLED	MORRIS	16
T.PRIME	RUN OUT		0
G.DODDS	BOWLED	MORRIS	23
S.CLEMENT	BOWLED	MORRIS	2
R.WILSON	NOT OUT		16
M.HADWIN	NOT OUT		5
		Extras	20
	Total (for 9 wkts)		152

Morecambe Bowling :

P.STEPHENS	8	0	16	1
R.MORRIS	8	1	36	3
F.PATEL	8	0	49	0
T.CLOUGH	8	1	19	1
G.PEDDER	8	1	28	0
A.BIRD	8	2	23	2

MORECAMBE

Batsman	How Out	Bowler	Runs
M.WOODHEAD	C.STRYDOM	CLEMENT	10
P.DENNISON	LBW	STRYDOM	59
R.MORRIS	C.WHITE	CLEMENT	30
P.THORNTON	C.WILSON	STRYDOM	12
B.LITTLE	RUN OUT		12
T.CLOUGH	C.PRIME	HADWIN	6
G.PEDDER	NOT OUT		18
A.BIRD	NOT OUT		0
		Extras	6
	Total (for 6 wkts)		153

Netherfield Bowling :

R.WILSON	8	0	40	0
C.WALMSLEY	7	0	41	0
S.CLEMENT	8	4	7	2
P.STRYDOM	8	3	24	2
M.HADWIN	7	1	39	1

FURNESS BUILDING SOCIETY CUP FINAL 2008

MORECAMBE V PRESTON

MORECAMBE

Batsman	How Out	Bowler		Runs
V.GOYAL	LBW	VAHALAWALA		10
M.WOODHEAD	C.JOHNSTONE	PAREKH		17
P.THORNTON	C.JOHNSTONE	DAVIES		21
P.DENNISON	C AND B	DAVIES		1
T.CLOUGH	C AND B	PAREKH		1
M.LOMAS	C.WILLIAMS	PATEL		1
B.MARTIN	NOT OUT			40
G.PEDDER	C.WILLIAMS	PAREKH		12
D.GUDGEON	RUN OUT			3
G.LEE	RUN OUT			8
J.GATES	NOT OUT			0
			Extras	8
			Total (for 9 wkts)	122

Preston Bowling :

B.ASAD	6 2 12 0
Y.PATEL	4 0 14 1
L.VAHALUWALA	8 4 16 1
M.BAVLA	6 0 26 0
J.DAVIES	8 1 38 2
M.PAREKH	8 2 13 3

PRESTON

Batsman	How Out	Bowler	Runs
M.BAVLA	BOWLED	GATES	2
S.PATEL	BOWLED	GATES	11
L.VAHALUWALA	LBW	GATES	14
B.ASAD	BOWLED	LEE	21
Y.PATEL	C.LOMAS	LEE	6
J.DAVIES	BOWLED	CLOUGH	11
J.McDONALD	C.GOYAL	CLOUGH	11
F.SAIYED	RUN OUT	GATES	3
M.PAREKH	NOT OUT		2
G.JOHNSTONE	LBW	MARTIN	6
C.WILLIAMS	BOWLED	CLOUGH	5
		Extras	25
		Total (for 10 wkts)	117

Morecambe Bowling :

J.GATES	8 1 21 3
G.LEE	8 3 15 2
G.PEDDER	7 0 29 0
T.CLOUGH	4.3 1 11 3
B.MARTIN	8 3 31 3

Advanced Subscribers

Gulam Maje
Byran Till
Ray Jagger
Michael Fisher
In Memory of Brian Fisher
Jack Read
Ricky Marsland
Nick Milner
Mr & Mrs J A & E Milner
Brendan Hetherington
Jim Hetherington
Dave Allison
Stan Barraclough
Tommy Clough
John Normanton
Gareth Pedder
Paul Speak
George Millican
Stuart Smith
John Cassidy
Iain Makinson
Andrew Speak
Ian Fisher
Mike Latham
Phil Thornton
Phil Dennison
Stuart McDonald
Duncan Hall
Darren Whittaker
Keith Whittaker
Scott Cockburn
James Vipond
Peter Stephens

Ian Ledward
Christopher Lamb
John Goodwin
Dave Pedder
Faruk Patel
Ian Gray
Brian Paton
Jim Stone
Colin Wilson
Roger Sandham
Mike Willis
Chris Till
Roy Crossley
Les Jones
Johnny Stewart
T P Aspinall & Son Ltd
Alan Butler
Bob Mashiter
Norman Hullay
Charles Clough
Mark Woodhead
Dave Derham
Mark Brzezinka
Alex Turner
Tim Smith
Tommy Hanley
Wiggy
Damian Gilhespy
Andy Devlin
Frank Errington
In memory of Geoff Bates from all the family
Jonathan Gates